KU-781-060

Publisher's Note:
All reasonable care has been exercised by the author and publisher to ensure that the tips and remedies included in this guide are simple and safe. However, it is important to note that all uses of vinegar should be practised with caution, and a doctor's, or relevant professional's, advice should be sought if in any doubt or before any topical or medicinal usage. Neither the editors, the author nor the publisher take responsibility for any consequences of any application which results from reading the information contained herein.

Please note also that the measurements provided in this book are presented as metric/imperial/US-cups practical equivalents, and that all eggs are medium (UK)/large (US) respectively unless otherwise stated.

Publisher and Creative Director: Nick Wells
Project Editor and Picture Research: Catherine Taylor
Special Photographer: Paul Forrester
Art Director: Mike Spender
Layout Design: Jane Ashley & Mike Spender
Operations Manager: Chris Herbert

Special thanks to Giana Porpiglia, Stephen Feather, Laura Bulbeck, Daniela Nava and Helen Snaith.

FLAME TREE PUBLISHING
6 Melbray Mews
Fulham, London SW6 3NS
United Kingdom

www.flametreepublishing.com

This edition first published in 2017
© 2017 this edition Flame Tree Publishing Ltd

17 19 21 20 18

1 3 5 7 9 10 8 6 4 2

ISBN 978-1-78664-534-0

All rights reserved. No part of this publication may be reproduced, stored in a retrieval system, or transmitted in any form or by any means, electronic, mechanical, photocopying, recording or otherwise, without prior permission in writing of the publisher.

Every effort has been made to contact copyright holders. We apologise in advance for any omissions and would be pleased to insert the appropriate acknowledgement in subsequent editions of this publication.

A CIP Record for this book is available from the British Library upon request.

Printed in China

Maria Costantino
& Gina Steer

Vinegar

100s of HOUSEHOLD USES

WITHDRAWN FROM STOCK

Maria Costantino
& Gina Steer

Vinegar

100s of HOUSEHOLD USES

WREXHAM C.B.C LIBRARY	
LLYFRGELL B.S. WRECSAM	
C56 0000 0645 283	
Askews & Holts	22-Aug-2017
640.41	£9.99
	WXMCOEDP

FLAME TREE
PUBLISHING

Contents

Introduction 6
Types of Vinegar. 12

Laundry. 28
Clean & Condition. .30
Ironing 48

Cleaning 52
All-purpose Solutions. 54
Kitchen. 60
Bathroom 70
Furnishings & Surfaces 76
Odour & Pest Control 86

Home Improvements 92
Do It Yourself 94

The Outdoors 104
Gardening. 106
Home Exteriors 116

Animal Care 124
Clean & Healthy .126

Health & Personal Care 134

Apple Cider Vinegar 136

Ailments & Problem Conditions 144

Improving Appearance .158

Cookery & Recipes. 170

The Basics 172

Flavoured Vinegars 180

Dressings, Sauces & Chutneys 188

Starters, Salads & Side Dishes 206

Main Courses 216

Desserts 228

Kids' Stuff. 236

Fun Science for Kids 238

Further Reading 250

Websites. 252

Picture Credits 253

Index 254

Introduction

History

Vinegar has been made and used for thousands of years: in fact, vinegar is the oldest storable food and because it can be stored for an almost unlimited period, it is the only food without an expiry date.

The ancient Babylonians around 5,000 BC were among the first to recognize the versatile nature of vinegar and used it as both a preserver and a condiment. They were also the first to flavour vinegar with herbs and spices. The 'Father of Medicine', Hippocrates (460–370 BC), is known to have prescribed vinegar to his patients in order to restore the four humours (blood, black bile, yellow bile and phlegm) to a balanced harmony.

Vinegar is also mentioned in the Bible – in the Book of Ruth and in Proverbs – and it was specified in the Talmud for making haroseth: a dried fruit and nut paste eaten at Passover as a reminder of the mortar used in buildings by the Israelites when they were slaves in Egypt.

An Expensive Dish

The Egyptian queen Cleopatra understood vinegar's solvent property: according to Pliny the Elder, Cleopatra bet her lover Mark Antony that she could spend 10 million sesterces on a single meal. Antony accepted the bet and the next night was surprised to be served a quite modest meal. He believed he had won the bet, when Cleopatra ordered the second course – a cup of vinegar – to be served. The queen, however, removed one of her pearl earrings, dropped it into the vinegar, watched it dissolve and then drank the mix.

A Military Staple

While citizens of Rome enjoyed fine wine, ordinary soldiers had to make do with posca, a mix of vinegar and water with a little honey as an optional extra. Vinegar also came in useful against the Romans: when the great Carthaginian general Hannibal and his army crossed the Alps on the back of elephants, any boulders that blocked their path were heated and doused with vinegar, causing the inconvenient obstacle to be shattered.

Medicinal Use Continues

In the nursery rhyme, when 'Jack fell down and broke his crown' he bound his head with vinegar and brown paper. The therapeutic benefits of vinegar have been known for centuries: in Asia, vinegar is known as the 'friend of Chinese herbs' because it is often used in the preparation of traditional medicines. During the American Civil War, vinegar was used to treat scurvy and as recently as the First World War it was being used in trench hospitals to sterilize wounds.

Whether you call them 'traditional', 'natural' or 'folk' remedies or recipes, today vinegar continues to be one of the most versatile products in the kitchen and medicine cabinet. And, with our growing awareness of the impact of chemicals on our environment, vinegar finds itself once more at the forefront of household cleaning.

Production

Vinegar is nothing more than an alcoholic beverage that has 'gone sour', which explains the French origins of the word *vin aigre*, meaning 'sour wine' – although it was not until 1864 that Louis Pasteur made sense of this natural process of fermentation. When alcoholic beverages sour, it is because of the action of certain bacteria, known as acetobacter, on the alcohol that turns it to acetic acid and water. Other elements, such as the type of fruit or grain from which the alcohol is originally made, give different vinegars their individual characteristic tastes, bodies and colours.

The Orleans Method

In theory, making vinegar is a very simple process: make some wine (or beer) and expose it to the air for the vinegar bacteria to get to work. The acetobacter reaction is an aerobic reaction and simply requires the presence of oxygen. One of the oldest methods for producing vinegar is called the Orleans process. The 'generator' used is a large wooden barrel that is laid on its side with the bunghole facing towards the top. At each end of the barrel, holes are drilled so that when the beer or dilute wine is put in, the liquid in the barrel is just below the holes. The slow fermentation allows for a non-toxic slime, known as the 'vinegar mother' composed of the bacteria and soluble cellulose, to form on top of the liquid. The barrel holes are covered with fine gauze (to keep out insects) and the generator allowed to sit for several months at around 87°F/29°C. When all the liquid is turned to vinegar, all but 15 per cent is drawn off through the bottom of the barrel. What is left behind in the barrel is the vinegar mother that becomes the 'starter' for the next batch of vinegar.

The more oxygen available in the process, the faster the vinegar can be made. So, over the centuries vinegar producers came up with a variety of ways of increasing the amount of oxygen in order to shorten the time taken in the vinegar-making process. Today, commercial vinegar is produced using either a fast or slow method: slow methods are used with traditional vinegars and can take several months. A form of nematode, known as a vinegar eel (*Turbatrix aceti*), that feeds on the vinegar mother can occur in some forms of vinegar – in particular, naturally fermenting vinegar – but most manufacturers filter and pasteurize their vinegar before bottling, thereby avoiding any adulteration.

Speedy Production

The fast methods of vinegar production generally add vinegar mother to the liquid and then introduce air using a turbine or pumping system. Additionally, the generator may be loosely packed with a porous material such as *pommace* (grape pulp after is has been pressed) or beech wood shavings to provide a 'mash' with a greater surface area for the volume of vinegar mother. This method can produce vinegar in 24 to 36 hours.

Activity Levels

The acetic acid concentration of vinegar typically ranges from four to eight per cent by volume for condiment (table) vinegar, though it is usually around the five per cent mark. It exists in much higher concentrations for pickling – up to 18 per cent – although in some countries the maximum strength may be less than this, as solutions above 10 per cent need careful handling because they are corrosive to the skin.

TYPES OF VINEGAR

White Distilled

White distilled vinegar – in fact colourless and transparent in appearance – is also sometimes called spirit vinegar and is produced by oxidizing a distilled alcohol made from grain (usually maize). White distilled vinegar is typically stronger and sharper than other vinegars and consequently is most often used in pickling and preserving recipes. Its stronger concentration of acetic acid also makes it a valuable household cleansing agent.

Malt Vinegar

Malt vinegar is made from a grain (typically barley). The barley is first softened by steeping in water and is then allowed to germinate. This causes the natural enzymes in the grain to become active and start digesting the starch that is converted into maltose, or sugar, before fermentation. The vinegar is then filtered and aged – often for some years – before bottling.

The distinctive flavour of malt vinegar makes it a popular choice for pickling and for sprinkling on fish and chips. A less expensive alternative is 'non-brewed condiment': this is typically a solution of acetic acid and citric acid coloured with caramel. Because it is non-brewed, it is a 'safe' vinegar for those who eschew all alcohol-based products.

Beer Vinegar

Vinegar made from beer, which is technically a malt vinegar, is a speciality of Germany, Austria and the Netherlands, and its flavour depends on the type of beer it is made from. In Bavaria, speciality beer vinegar continues to be made according to the Bavarian Law of Purity of 1516 enacted by Duke Wilhelm IV, and which requires all beer and beer products to be made solely of barley, hops and water. Like the beers themselves, continental beer vinegars are lighter in colour than British ales and malt vinegar, although they do all share the distinctive 'malty' taste.

Red & White Wine Vinegar

Wine vinegar is made from either red or white grapes, and like wine itself, it is the variety of grape used that defines the flavour. Also like wine, there are different qualities of wine vinegar available. Generally, the longer wine vinegar is aged, the better the quality – the finest quality often being aged for two years. Because red wine vinegar has a strong, full bodied flavour, it is most commonly used in Mediterranean cookery recipes for marinades and vinaigrettes.

Made from selected blends of white wine, white wine vinegar can vary in colour from 'white' to pale gold. White wine vinegar has an acid content of between five and seven per cent and therefore a sharper flavour than red wine vinegar.

Champagne Vinegar

With a taste similar to champagne, this vinegar is produced using the same grape varieties as the 'king of wines', Chardonnay and Pinot Noir. The same process for making wine

vinegar is used, but once the grape hulls are removed and the liquid drained, the end result is a fine vinegar with the rich flavour of champagne along with a hint of vanilla, which comes from the aged oak barrels in which this vinegar is made.

Balsamic Vinegar

True balsamic vinegar comes only from Modena and Reggio Emilia in Italy and is made from the juice of Trebbiano and Spergola grapes. The traditional method of production involves an initial fermentation which reduces the volume of the 'juice' by two thirds, and then the thickened 'storm' is placed in the first of a series of five barrels made only of approved woods: oak, chestnut, cherry, ash and juniper. At each barrelling, the volume of liquid has been reduced: from an initial 100 litres (26 gallons), to 70, then 50, to 30 and finally, a mere 10-litre barrel of dark – almost black – viscous and sweet-flavoured vinegar.

After five years the first balsamic vinegar is ready, but only balsamic vinegar that has been aged for at least 12 years – and up to 150 years – may be labelled *Aceto Balsamico Tradizionale*. It is this long, slow method of 'hand' production that accounts for the typically high price of traditional balsamic vinegar. Industrialized production using grape concentrate, sugar, caramel (to darken the colour) and wood flavourings makes for cheaper, but inferior, balsamic-'type' vinegars.

Sherry Vinegar

Like balsamic vinegar, sherry vinegar is a speciality of a distinct geographical region and production method. To be called sherry, the fortified wine may only be made in the Spanish province of Cadiz, and in a defined area between Jerez, Sanlúcar de Barrameda and El Puerto de Santa Maria.

Made in the region since the sixteenth century, the wine must be made by the *solera* system (a fractional blending method) and aged for at least two years. The vinegar itself comes from barrels of sherry that contain too much volatile acidity, so cannot be used for wine. Like balsamic vinegar, the longer sherry vinegar is aged, the finer the quality: 30-, 50- and 75-year-old *reserva* sherry vinegars are highly prized for their rich, mellow flavours.

Apple Cider Vinegar

Made from cider or from an apple must or 'mash', cider vinegar has a strong, acid-sharp flavour at full strength, but when dilute, has a distinctive apple taste. Fast industrial manufacture, which can take as little as 24 hours, often uses concentrated juice from eating or dessert apples with added sugar, rather than traditional Somerset cider apple varieties, such as Kingston Black, Morgan Sweet, Sheep's Nose and Yarlington Mill, which are fermented naturally for at least two years. Such cider vinegars are a brownish-yellow colour, and are often sold unfiltered and so contain vinegar mother.

Rice Vinegar

Rice vinegar is a speciality of China, Japan and Southeast Asia, and comes in white (actually a pale yellow), black and red varieties. White rice vinegar is made from fermented rice, although a variant with a stronger taste, and often called seasoned rice vinegar, is made from Japanese rice wine or sake.

Black rice vinegar, usually made from sweet black rice but which can also use millet and sorghum, is a dark brown colour and has a distinctive smoky taste, while red rice vinegar is made from fermented red yeast rice and has a sweet but salty flavour, which makes it ideal for use in sweet-and-sour dishes and dipping sauces.

Fruit Vinegar

Fruit vinegars are made from fruit wines with no other flavours added – not to be confused with non-fruit vinegars infused with fruit or with added fruit flavours. The most common fruit vinegars are those made with raspberries, blueberries or blackberries, which are consequently sweet and delicately flavoured. Many fruit vinegars are specialities of Europe, although fruits such as persimmon and apple-flavoured *jujube* (Chinese date) are used in Korea and China.

Raisin Vinegar

This cloudy brown, mildly flavoured vinegar is sometimes also called grape vinegar – raisins are, after all, dried grapes. Raisin vinegar is produced widely in Greece and Turkey.

Date Vinegar

We know the Babylonians in around 5000 BC were making vinegar and it was most likely made from dates, the only available staple foodstuff for the inhabitants of desert and arid regions. Both raisin and date vinegars are popular in Middle Eastern cuisine.

Umezu

The famous Japanese 'pickled plums' (actually apricots!) called *umeboshi* are the source of *ume* vinegar or *umezu*: the fruits are picked when ripe, packed in barrels with salt and a weighted lid placed on top. Gradually, the *ume* plums give up their juice and the salty liquid is drawn off and marketed as *umezu* or vinegar.

Coconut Vinegar

Used extensively in Southeast Asian cooking, especially in Thai cuisine, and made from the 'tuba' or 'toddy' – the sap of the coconut palm – coconut vinegar has a low acidity, a slightly musty flavour and a unique aftertaste. The sap is naturally fermented into vinegar over 45 to 60 days, then bottled. Unfiltered and unpasteurized coconut vinegar contains vinegar mother, and as it ages in the bottle, the colour changes from cloudy white, to light yellow, to clear light brown. Filtered and pasteurized versions are also available.

Honey Vinegar

Honey is often added to vinegar – especially cider vinegar – to enhance the flavour, but vinegars made from honey are also produced, particularly in France and Italy. Fermented honey, water and yeast were used for thousands of years to make a traditional wine called mead and the resulting honey vinegar is gold coloured, lightly flavoured but highly aromatic.

Cane Vinegar

In the Ilocos region of the northern Philippines where this vinegar is traditionally made, it is known as *sukang iloko*. Outside of the Philippines, it is often labelled as *sukang massim*, which simply

translates as 'sour vinegar'. Although it is made from sugar cane juice, it is no sweeter than other vinegars and has a rich, sharp flavour that makes it ideal for pickles and sauces.

Corn Sugar Vinegar

Corn sugar vinegar is the result of alcoholic and then subsequent acetous fermentation of corn sugar. It has a smooth, mild flavour and distinctive amber colour.

Kombucha Vinegar

Sometimes called 'pro-biotic vinegar', kombucha vinegar is made from a colony of yeast and acetic acid bacteria which forms into a 'mat'. This culture also goes by the acronym SCOBY (Symbiotic Colony of Bacteria and Yeast) and was originally made into fermented 'tea' during the Qin Dynasty in China around 250 BC and used extensively in traditional Chinese medicine.

Each time the kombucha colony is fermented, a new colony is produced and forms a new layer on top of the mat. After three or four layers have built up, the 'tea' becomes sour and tastes like vinegar. Both the kombucha tea and the vinegar have recently become very popular on account of their alleged therapeutic properties.

Flavoured Vinegars

Flavoured vinegars are, as their name implies, vinegars that have had flavours added to them rather than made from them. Generally the 'base vinegar' is a red or white wine vinegar in which fruits, such as raspberries, lemons, oranges (especially the deep red blood orange) and even figs, have been infused. Herbs and spices are also popular flavourings: thyme, oregano, rosemary, tarragon, basil, mustard, chilli and garlic can all be used. (See pages 180–87.)

LAUNDRY

Clean & Condition

The level of acetic acid in white or distilled vinegar is strong enough to dissolve the alkalis in soaps and detergents, but not strong enough to harm fabrics – and it has bactericidal properties. Consequently, white vinegar is a valuable 'green' alternative to synthetic cleaners and when it is diluted with water, which further reduces the risk to delicate fabrics, it is also a very economical one. It is also useful for keeping the colour fast in laundry and is a great way to put the 'bounce' back into fibres.

Cleaning Clothes

Pre-wash Stain Removal

White vinegar is such a useful pre-wash stain remover that it is worthwhile keeping a spray bottle with a half-and-half solution of white vinegar and water close to hand. As you check over garments before putting them in the washer, treat any heavy grime or underarm perspiration stains with a quick spray of vinegar.

Wine Stains

Wine stains can be removed from cotton and cotton polyester fabrics – but only if you get to the stain within 24 hours! Here you do need to use undiluted white vinegar: sponge it gently on to the stained area and blot with a clean cloth. Repeat until as much of the wine stain as possible has been removed and then wash according to the care label instructions for the garment.

Deodorant Stains

Antiperspirants and deodorants can leave horrible white marks on clothes. These can be removed by lightly rubbing white vinegar on them and then laundering as usual.

Soak Away Bloodstains

Bloodstains are quite easy to remove before they have dried and set into fabric but are nearly impossible to shift after 24 hours. If you can get to the bloodstain quickly, pour

undiluted white vinegar directly onto the spot and let it soak in for 5–10 minutes before blotting with a clean cloth. Repeat if necessary and then launder as usual.

Unset Old Stains

Older, set-in stains can be successfully removed by treating the affected area with a solution of 3 tablespoons white vinegar, 2 tablespoons liquid detergent and 1 litre/2 pints/4½ cups warm water. Repeatedly sponge and blot the stained area, and then launder.

Collars and Cuffs

Collars and cuffs are particularly vulnerable to stains, especially greasy ones from perfumes (sprayed on the pulse points of the neck and wrists) and from make-up.

Make a paste of 2 parts white vinegar and 3 parts bicarbonate of soda (baking soda) and use a soft nail brush – or a discarded and recycled toothbrush – to gently brush the paste into the soiled cuffs and collars. Let the paste set on the fabric for half an hour and then launder as usual. This technique is also good for removing mildew spots from vintage fabrics.

 CAUTION: Don't forget to be gentle when applying vinegar to clothes – too much rubbing away might damage delicate fabrics!

Ink Spots

The primary carrier for the colour in ball-point and roller-ball pen inks is a very fine oil – often castor oil – so ink marks can be treated with white vinegar, which cuts through the grease and lets the colour flow off the affected fabric.

Treat the ink stain first by blotting with undiluted white vinegar, and then gently rub in a paste of 2 parts white vinegar and 3 parts cornflour (cornstarch). Let the paste dry completely on the ink stain and then launder as usual.

Better than Bleach

Greying white socks, and even dingy face flannels, can be made brighter and given an antibacterial treatment: place about 1.7 litres/3 pints/7¼ cups cold water and about 145 ml/5 fl oz/⅔ cup white vinegar into a large saucepan and bring it to the boil. Put the dingy socks – or face flannels – into a bucket and pour the boiling vinegar solution over them. Let them soak overnight and, the next day, launder them as usual.

Restore Whites

White garments or fabrics that have yellowed can be returned to their former glory by soaking them overnight in a solution of 12 parts warm water and 1 part white vinegar and then laundered the following day as usual.

Vintage Lace Restored

Old and antique lace is often very delicate so start any cleaning process by soaking it first in cold water and letting it dry naturally.

If it is still on the yellow side when dry, use a very mild solution of white vinegar and water: 24 parts water and 1 part white vinegar for an overnight soak. Rinse well and allow the lace to dry naturally – in the sun if possible, as this will also help in the 'bleaching' process.

Banish Smells from Suits

A night out can leave your clothes smelling of stale cigarette smoke or even of the food you ate in the restaurant. You can, however, often remove the odour from clothes without resorting to dry cleaning. Put 145 ml/5 fl oz/⅔ cup white vinegar in the bathtub and fill the tub with hot water. Hang the offending garments in your bathroom and close the door, and let the 'vinegar steam' impregnate and deodorize the garments for a couple of hours.

 CAUTION: Afterwards, hang the garments in an open space – not the wardrobe – to let them 'dry out'.

Second-hand Smells

Scouring vintage and second-hand clothing stores can yield fashionable finds, but even though the garments may have been cleaned, they can often have lingering odours. Add 120 ml/4 fl oz/½ cup

white vinegar to the wash cycle – or to a bathtub of water if the garment is vintage and needs delicate hand washing. This will deodorize the garment and kill off any bacteria that may be present.

Kill Bacteria

Because of the acetic acid content, white vinegar has bactericidal properties and so about 120 ml/4 fl oz/½ cup white vinegar added to your washer's rinse cycle will kill off any bacteria present in the wash load, especially if it contains terry diapers (or sweaty sports socks). White vinegar will naturally break down uric acid from baby and children's clothes.

Clean Machine

You will not get clean clothes from a dirty washing machine, so once in a while, pour in about 230 ml/8 fl oz/ 1 cup white vinegar and run the washer on a full cycle but without clothes or detergents. This will clean out residual soap scum, remove mineral deposits and deodorize your washing machine.

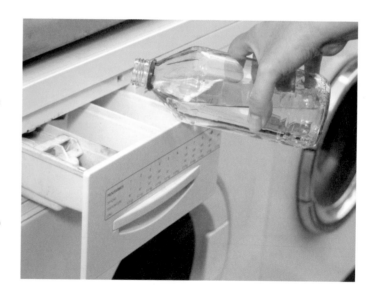

Blanket Reviver

Cotton and wool blankets and bedding can be revived and made soft and fluffy – and free of soap residues and odours – by adding about 230 ml/8 fl oz/1 cup white vinegar to the final rinse cycle.

No More Fabric Softeners

Unless you happen to like your laundry smelling of synthetic perfumes, there is no need for expensive fabric softening liquids or sheets (the latter are also partly responsible for 'furring up' the heating elements of washing machines, causing them to overheat and break down!). Instead, try adding 120 ml/ 4 fl oz/½ cup white vinegar to the final rinse for soft and fresh-smelling clothes.

Lint-free Laundry

If your clothes are emerging from the wash covered in lint, do not despair. Next time, add some white vinegar to the final rinse and you will find them l int-free – and static-free too.

Banish Wrinkles

Sometimes clothes have wrinkles and creases that have dried in: this can happen even when they are brand new from the store. Rather than iron them out, de-wrinkle them by hanging the garment on a clothes hanger and lightly spraying a mist of a solution of 1 part white vinegar and 3 parts water. Let the garment air-dry.

Shiny Seats

The seats of skirts and trousers can become shiny, even after a single wear. Dip an old, but clean, toothbrush into a solution of equal parts white vinegar and water, and gently brush the shiny area. Blot the moisture with a clean towel and let the garment air-dry.

Suede Stains

Grease spots on suede garments, shoes and handbags can be removed if you dip a clean toothbrush into neat white vinegar and very gently brush the spot. Do not scrub or you will damage the nap. Let the spot air-dry then brush with a suede brush and repeat if required. Suede items can be generally revived by a gentle wipe over with a sponge dipped in white vinegar.

Salt Marks

Shoes and boots are so easily spoiled in winter when the roads have been gritted with rock salt. Not only does this leave an ugly tide mark on footwear, but the salt can cause leather, suede and fabric to crack if it is not removed. As soon as you can, wipe off fresh salt stains with a sponge dipped in undiluted white vinegar and let the shoes dry naturally.

Colour Maintenance

Keep Colours Fast

New and old coloured garments can lose much of their colour in the wash and you can end up with faded or streaky patches. To fix the colour, soak coloured fabrics and garments for a few minutes in a bowl of diluted white vinegar before you wash them.

Stop Red Running

Red is a notorious colour for running in the wash and turning everything washed with it pink. However pre-soaking a new red item in undiluted white vinegar before the first wash can limit the amount of red dye that is shed.

 CAUTION: It is still a good idea to wash dark and coloured items separately from white items, but you will find the red items do not lose as much of their colour in the long run.

Bright White, Sparkling Colours

Whiter whites can be had without the use of chlorine beach or the expensive 'bleaches' designed for coloured garments – use white vinegar in the rinse cycle instead. The effect is the same: it fixes the dye, cleans, deodorizes and softens – all in one treatment.

Ironing

As the final stage in the laundry process, ironing gives garments the finishing touch. Remember, though, that there are two ironing techniques: the first is truly ironing, where the sole of the iron is passed gently across the top of the garment to remove creases, and the second is pressing, where the sole of the iron is pressed onto the garment to bring it back into shape and 'iron in' creases. In either case, white vinegar can have a part to play.

Flush Out Your Iron

Clean out your steam iron by filling the reservoir with undiluted white vinegar. Place the iron in an upright position, switch it on to the steam setting and let the vinegar steam clean the interior for 10–15 minutes. This will get rid of any mineral deposits and help prevent the insides corroding. Next, repeat with clean water to flush out any leftover vinegar.

Spotless Sole

Take a look at the soleplate of your iron: are there black scorch marks? If there are, you can guarantee that the next time you iron your favourite garment, these will get deposited onto the fabric! When the iron is cold, scrub the soleplate with a paste made of equal parts of warmed white vinegar and salt, and then clean off with a cloth dampened in clean water.

Remove Scorch Marks

Small, slight scorch marks on clothing will often come out if you rub the spot with a clean cloth dampened in white vinegar and then blot with a clean cloth, repeating if necessary. This technique can work on rust spots too!

Stay Sharp

Some garments demand razor sharp creases, so use a spray diffuser with a solution of equal parts white vinegar and water, and lightly spray the garment before ironing. For some reason, the creases are even sharper if you place a piece of brown paper on the garment and iron onto this rather than directly onto the fabric. Try it for yourself!

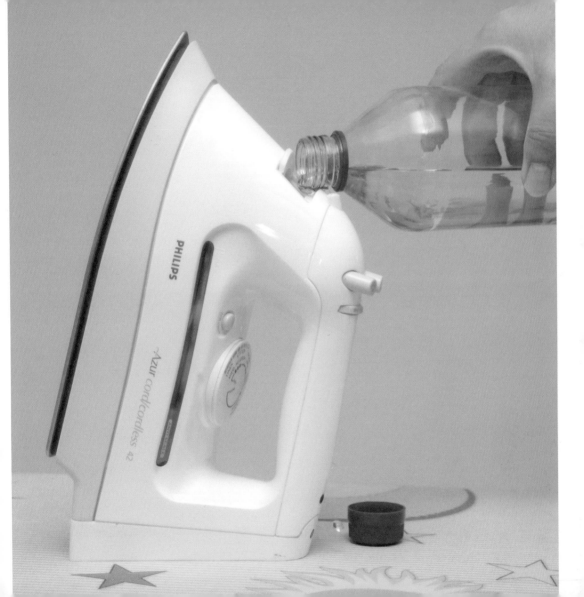

CLEANING

All-purpose Solutions

As a cleaning substance, white vinegar makes an excellent, economical and eco-friendly alternative to many chemical cleansers. The acetic acid content is enough to cut through grease and grime, but it is also bactericidal, making it effective against most moulds, bacteria and germs. Here you will see a varied selection of basic all-purpose solutions and tips.

All-purpose Metal Cleaner

Go to the household store and you will find an expensive array of different scourers, polishes and cleaners labelled for chrome, steel or copper. There is no need to spend money on different products when you can make an effective all-round metal cleaner yourself for a few pennies – and be safe in the knowledge that you are not harming the environment.

Mix a tablespoon of ordinary cooking salt and a tablespoon of flour (self-raising or plain!) with a little white vinegar to make a paste. Work the paste around the surface to be cleaned, then rinse with warm water.

Brass, Pewter and Copper Polish

Make metal ornaments and door furniture shine by polishing with a mixture of 2 tablespoons tomato ketchup and 1 tablespoon white vinegar. Rub on with a cloth until bright and shiny.

Cleaner for Gold Jewellery

There is no need for expensive cleaners; just submerge gold jewellery in apple cider vinegar for 10 minutes, then rinse off and dry.

 CAUTION: This is only suitable for plain gold items, not jewellery set with gemstones!

Remove Candle Wax

Candles give a gorgeous light and scented candles are a wonderful way to perfume a room. Apart from the fire risk, the only other problem with candles is that they can splutter molten wax onto walls and furniture.

 CAUTION: Rather than scrape off the wax with a knife or blade, which may damage the surface underneath, heat it gently first with a hair dryer and blot up as much molten wax as you can with paper towels.

Next, tackle the greasy marks by mopping them with a clean rag soaked in a solution of equal parts white vinegar and water, and then blot with a clean, dry cloth.

Un-stick Stickers

Trying to remove the stuck-on price tags from new china and glassware – or from any other object – is probably one of the most frustrating and time-consuming activities on the planet. You can peel, poke and rub away, and still there are bits that will not shift.

Thankfully, there is a straightforward method: saturate the sticker with undiluted white vinegar and scrape it off. Do not use your fingernail: it will only break! Try using a plastic knife for small, delicate objects so that you do not scratch the surface, or an expired credit or phone card for larger surfaces. If there are any sticky leftovers, saturate again with vinegar and wipe clean with a cloth.

This method works equally well for those sticky decals that are popular with young children and notices on car windows left by traffic wardens.

Kitchen

Cooking is a messy business but kitchens need to be clean and hygienic so that food prepared in them tastes delicious and is safe to eat. The antibacterial properties of vinegar make it an ideal surface cleanser for food preparation surfaces: undiluted white vinegar at five per cent acidity is effective against *E. Coli*, *Salmonella* and *Staphylococcus*, so make vinegar part of your cleaning routine.

Kitchen Items & Surfaces

Clean China and Glass

Make your dinner service sparkle by adding a splash of white vinegar to your rinse water or dishwasher. Cloudy glasses can be made clear again if you soak them for 10–15 minutes in a solution of equal parts hot water and white vinegar, and scrub with a soft bottle brush.

Tea- and coffee-stained cups and mugs can be restored by scrubbing with equal parts vinegar and salt followed by a rinse in warm water.

Grease Stains

The reason we sprinkle vinegar on our fish and chips is not just because it tastes good, but because it cuts through the grease, making the food easier to digest. Tackle grease marks and splatters on surfaces around the home with a cloth dampened in a solution of equal parts white wine vinegar and water. Not only will it get rid of the grease, the vinegar will also remove any lingering 'fatty smells' – once its own scent has evaporated.

Cutting Boards

Vinegar is effective against harmful bugs, such as E. Coli, *Salmonella* and *Staphylococcus*, so clean down wooden and

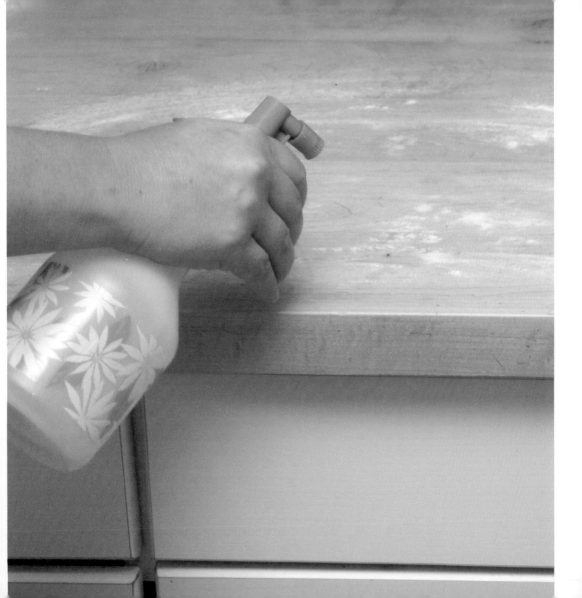

plastic cutting boards, butcher blocks and non-marble counter tops where food preparation takes place with undiluted white vinegar before and after use. If wooden surfaces need deodorizing after, sprinkle them with bicarbonate of soda (baking soda) and spray on some vinegar. Let it foam for a couple of minutes, then rinse with clean water.

Grill Pans

It is the grease that has dripped from food into the grill pan that smells when you next heat the grill up. Too much accumulated grease in a grill pan can also catch fire! Lining the pan with cooking foil is one way of keeping an eye on things, but even then you still need to clean out the pan to get rid of spill, splatters, odours and bacteria. A solution of equal parts white vinegar and warm water should do the job, but for really greasy pans, use neat vinegar or make a paste of vinegar and salt or bicarbonate of soda (baking soda) and get scrubbing.

Can Openers

Ever looked really close at the sharp point of the opener or at the cogged wheel? Be horrified at the amount of gunk that is lurking there! Every time you open a can some of that gunk will end up deposited on the surface of the food inside the can! Clean and disinfect your can opener by immersing it in undiluted white vinegar and scrubbing the mechanism with a re-cycled toothbrush.

Clean and Deodorize Food Containers

Plastic food containers, lunch boxes, bento boxes and vacuum flasks can be stained and scented by strong foods and liquids. Wash food containers in a solution of equal parts white

vinegar and water, and then rinse clean. Store with the lids off. If odours persist, place a slice of bread soaked in white vinegar in the food container (lid on) overnight: the smell should have gone by the next day.

Fresher Flasks

Vacuum flasks can get stained and smelly so clean them out regularly by filling with warm water and 120 ml/4 fl oz/½ cup white vinegar and letting them sit for a couple of hours. Any residue can be 'scoured' away by adding a small handful of uncooked rice. Put the lid on the flask and shake well, then rinse and let it air-dry.

Berry Stains

Preparing soft fruits can leave your hands – and food preparation surfaces – stained. Washing surfaces, bowls and hands with white vinegar and rinsing well with water afterwards will remove the stains.

Disinfect Dishcloths

Cleaning a surface is useless if the dishcloth, sponge or brush is itself dirty. Soak them after each use in neat white vinegar and hot water for a few minutes, then rinse and let dry. You can also soak loofahs and natural bath sponges in vinegar to clean them of soap residue. Rinse them off with clean water, and then revive them with a soak in a salt-water solution (which removes any 'slime') before giving them a final rinse in cold water.

Appliances

Fresh Fridge

Equal parts of white vinegar and water make an effective and safe cleaner for both the inside and outside of fridges. If you have got mould or mildew lurking in shelves and fridge drawers, zap them with undiluted white vinegar. An egg-cup-full of bicarbonate of soda (baking soda) placed in the fridge will help absorb odours too!

Kettle De-scaler

Lime and mineral deposits that have built up in kettles – and in coffee makers – can be shifted by boiling up – or brewing up – enough white vinegar to fill the pot to ¾ full for 5 minutes. Leave the vinegar in the kettle or coffee maker overnight then rinse out with cold water.

Clean Dishwashers and Microwaves

Once a month, remove soap build-up from dishwashers by pouring 120 ml/4 fl oz/½ cup white vinegar into the bottom of the unit – or placed in a bowl on the top rack. Run the machine on full cycle without dishes or detergent. Steam clean and deodorize your microwave with a shallow bowl of equal parts vinegar and water and set on high for 5 minutes. When cool, use the solution to wipe away splatters from the inside surfaces.

Bathroom

Relaxing in a tub of bubbles at the end of a hard day or waking up with an invigorating shower should be a pleasurable experience in pleasant surroundings. No matter how old your bathroom and its fittings, keeping it clean, bacteria- and odour-free will add to your sense of wellbeing.

Shower Curtains

If mildew has stained your shower curtain, wash it in warm water with equal parts laundry detergent and bicarbonate of soda (baking soda), and then rinse with 120 ml/4 fl oz/½ cup white vinegar added to the rinse water.

 CAUTION: If you use a washing machine, take the curtain out before the spin cycle so it does not crease. Hang the curtain back up and let it air-dry.

Shiny Showers

Soapy watermarks are unsightly on shower cubicles and screens, and if you live in a hard water area, they can be permanently etched into the 'glass' and ruin its clean looks. At the end of your shower, wipe them down with a solution of equal parts water and white vinegar. Finally, remove all traces of water and vinegar with a squeegee, and leave the shower door open to air-dry. Tackle sliding shower door tracks by pouring in neat white vinegar to clean and disinfect. Leave it to sit overnight and then mop out with a dry sponge.

Tiles and Grout

Soap, shampoo, shower gel and bath foam inevitably get splashed on tiles. Bring dull tiles back to brightness by washing them with a solution of 120 ml/4 fl oz/½ cup white vinegar in 1 litre/2 pints/4 cups warm water.

Tile grout loses its whiteness and turns grey with age and dirt over time, but its rough surface and porous nature also make it an ideal home for bacteria to thrive. A recycled toothbrush or nailbrush dipped in neat white vinegar will kill germs and whiten the grout.

Sinks and Tubs

Tide marks should be much easier to scrub away after a two-hour soak with hot water and a generous amount of white vinegar filled to a level just above the mark.

Unclog Plugholes

Soap, shower gel and bath oil residues and hair can build up in plugholes. Pour 4–5 tablespoons bicarbonate of soda (baking soda) into the plughole using a funnel. Next, pour in 120 ml/4 fl oz/½ cup white vinegar. When the fizzing stops, flush through with very hot water. Wait 5 minutes and then flush with cold water. This also kills odour-creating bacteria.

Shift Minerals from Shower Heads and Taps

Limescale deposits can quickly clog up the holes in shower heads, putting pressure on your hot water system. Hand-held shower heads can be immersed easily in a deep bowl of white vinegar and very hot water, and left to sit. The vinegar will dissolve and shift the deposits.

Fixed shower heads – and taps – are a bit more tricky: fill a plastic bag with neat white vinegar and fasten it with tape, string and rubber bands over the shower head or tap. Let sit in the vinegar for an hour or so, and then rinse off with cold water.

Toilet Bowls

An effective and economical way to keep your toilet bowl disinfected is to pour about 600 ml/1 pint/2½ cups white vinegar slowly over the sides of the bowl last thing at night. A once-a-week treatment should also help keep away the marks that appear above the water line.

Furnishings & Surfaces

Before mass-produced, industrial chemicals were made available to the

domestic market, homeowners made use of natural, organic products

that cleaned, protected and polished their furnishings without spending a

fortune or harming the environment. Antique furniture and furnishings have

lasted for so long looking beautiful because they were cared for very simply,

using the most basic products.

Furniture

Scratches in Wood

Unsightly scratches on wooden surfaces can be disguised using a little white or apple cider vinegar mixed in a jar with some iodine. Adjust the colour to match the wood – more vinegar for light woods, more iodine for dark woods – and paint the scratch mark carefully with an artists' paintbrush.

Water Rings

A wet glass on a wooden table inevitably leaves a white ring mark. These can be removed by a mixture of equal parts white vinegar and olive oil applyed with a soft cloth. Do not rub in circles, but move the cloth along the grain of the wood. Use a second clean cloth to polish up to a shine.

Wax and Polish Build-up

When furniture polish or wax builds up on surfaces, you can remove it easily and without damaging the underlying

wood with a mixture of equal proportions of white vinegar and water. Dip a cloth into the mix and wring it out well; then, moving in the direction of the grain of the wood, clean off the polish. Wipe dry with a soft, clean cloth.

Leather Furniture

Unsightly white water marks on leather furniture can also be removed by dabbing them with a sponge dipped in undiluted white vinegar.

Leather that has lost its shine can be revitalized with a mixture of equal parts of white vinegar and boiled linseed oil (available form art shops and hardware stores). Put the solution into a spray bottle and spray onto the leather. Spread it over the surface gently with a soft cloth and give it a minute or so to nourish the leather, then buff with a clean cloth.

Leather-topped tables are best cleaned by wiping with a soft cloth dipped in a solution of 2 parts water and 1 part white vinegar and dried off with a soft, clean cloth.

 CAUTION: Vinegar – and other acidic products – are NOT recommended for marble. This natural stone is made of calcium carbonate deposits and is 'soft', so its polished surface can be damaged even with the most 'mild' acid. Even wine glasses placed on a marble surface can etch rings, so use coasters!

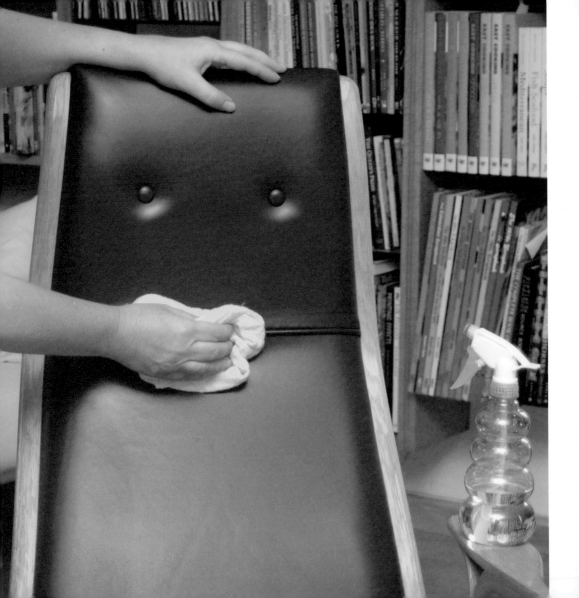

Windows & Floors

Let There Be Light

This is the tried and trusted method for getting windows (and mirrors) squeaky clean – it is also cheap and it keeps flies away too! Mix up equal parts of water and white vinegar in a spray bottle. Spray onto the glass and clean off the dirt with scrunched up newspaper. Finish off with a light polish with some brown paper.

Paint Splashes on Windows

Dribbles of dried-on paint on windows look unsightly but can be hard to remove without scratching the glass. The easy solution is to 'paint' undiluted hot white vinegar onto the mark and give it time to soften up before scraping off with a razor-edged tool.

Venetian Blinds

The horizontal slats of plastic or wooden Venetian blinds are notorious for collecting dirt, dust and grime. Wearing a cotton glove – or even an old sports sock placed over your hand – moistened at the end with a solution of equal parts white vinegar and warm water, run your hand across both sides of the blind slats to clean. You will be amazed at how much dirt is removed, so periodically you will have to rinse out the glove.

Carpet Stains

Some carpet stains can be removed with a paste made from 2 tablespoons white vinegar and 4 tablespoons bicarbonate of soda (baking soda) or ordinary cooking salt. Test on an inconspicuous part of the carpet first for colour fastness, and if it is safe, gently work the paste into the stained area: do not rub outwards as this will spread the stain. Instead, work from the edge of the stain towards the middle. Let the paste dry and the next day vacuum or brush up the powder residue.

 CAUTION: Do not forget to test on an inconspicuous part of the carpet first!

Vinyl and Lino Floors

Bring the shine back to a vinyl floor without making it slippery by washing it with a solution of 120 ml/4 fl oz/½ cup white vinegar to each 4 litre/1 gallon bucket of water. Many stains can be safely removed from linoleum floor covering by applying a splash of white vinegar, sprinkling bicarbonate of soda (baking soda) on top and rubbing gently. Rinse clean with water afterwards.

Odour & Pest Control

An often difficult task is trying to 'clean the air' of stale smoke and food odours; conventional chemical room fresheners simply mask the smell and are often overwhelming in themselves. Worse still, they simply shout out loud that your home smells and you have tried to hide the fact! Sniff out smells and deal with them using some simple solutions.

Smoke and Cooking Smells

Burned your dinner? Fried some fish? Had a great party? Banish lingering smells by placing bowls of neat white vinegar around the house. Smells will disappear in a day. Clear cigarette smoke from the air by flapping a tea towel moistened in white vinegar around the room! Preparing fish and strong smelling produce like garlic and onions can leave your hands – and food preparation surfaces – smelly. White vinegar will remove the odours from surfaces, but before you handle fish or cut vegetables, try wiping your hands with vinegar; it will make it easier to remove the odour afterwards.

Freshen Closets

A musty smelling closet needs cleaning and airing out – otherwise your clothes will smell the same! Take out all the contents of your closet, and then, wearing rubber gloves to protect your skin, wash down the walls, ceiling and floor with a cloth dampened in a solution of 120 ml/4 fl oz/½ cup white vinegar, 120 ml/4 fl oz/½ cup ammonia and 4 tablespoons bicarbonate of soda (baking soda) mixed in a bucket with 4 litres/1 gallon of water.

 CAUTION: Let the closet dry out completely before returning the contents.

If a smell persists, try placing a tray of clean cat litter on the floor to absorb the scent – and any residual moisture – and replenish every couple of days until the odour has disappeared.

Deodorize Footwear

Training shoes can be particularly smelly, so try this tip. Most sports shoes are machine washable, so before you put them in the machine, soak them for a few minutes in

a bucket with a solution of equal parts white vinegar and water. This will deodorize them and kill any bacteria that have taken up residence. Do the same for sports socks too, and check out the Health & Personal Care section for advice on 'fungal feet' to break the vicious cycle of foot odour.

Missing the Point

Vinegar breaks down uric acid so is a great way to deal with little accidents. Clean, disinfect and deodorize urine-splashed surfaces with a solution of equal parts white vinegar and water. Then sprinkle the area with bicarbonate of soda (baking soda) and let it dry. Brush or vacuum the powder residue after it is dry to the touch.

Fruit Flies

Eating five portions of fruit and vegetables a day is highly recommended, but that can mean a lot of fresh produce ripening in your kitchen: a welcome sign for fruit flies to come in and dine. Forget chemical fly-sprays; make a simple, eco-friendly fruit fly trap: half fill a conserve jar with apple cider vinegar, punch a couple of holes in the lid, screw it on and leave it for the flies to end their days in. Every so often, empty the vinegar away and give the flies a 'decent burial'.

Look What the Cat Dragged In

If Kitty has been hunting and brought home a mouse, clean the area thoroughly with neat white vinegar after you have retrieved the mouse remains. If it smells a little 'mousey' still, a neat trick is to lay a paper towel on the spot and put a dollop of washing-up liquid, shower gel or even shampoo on it.

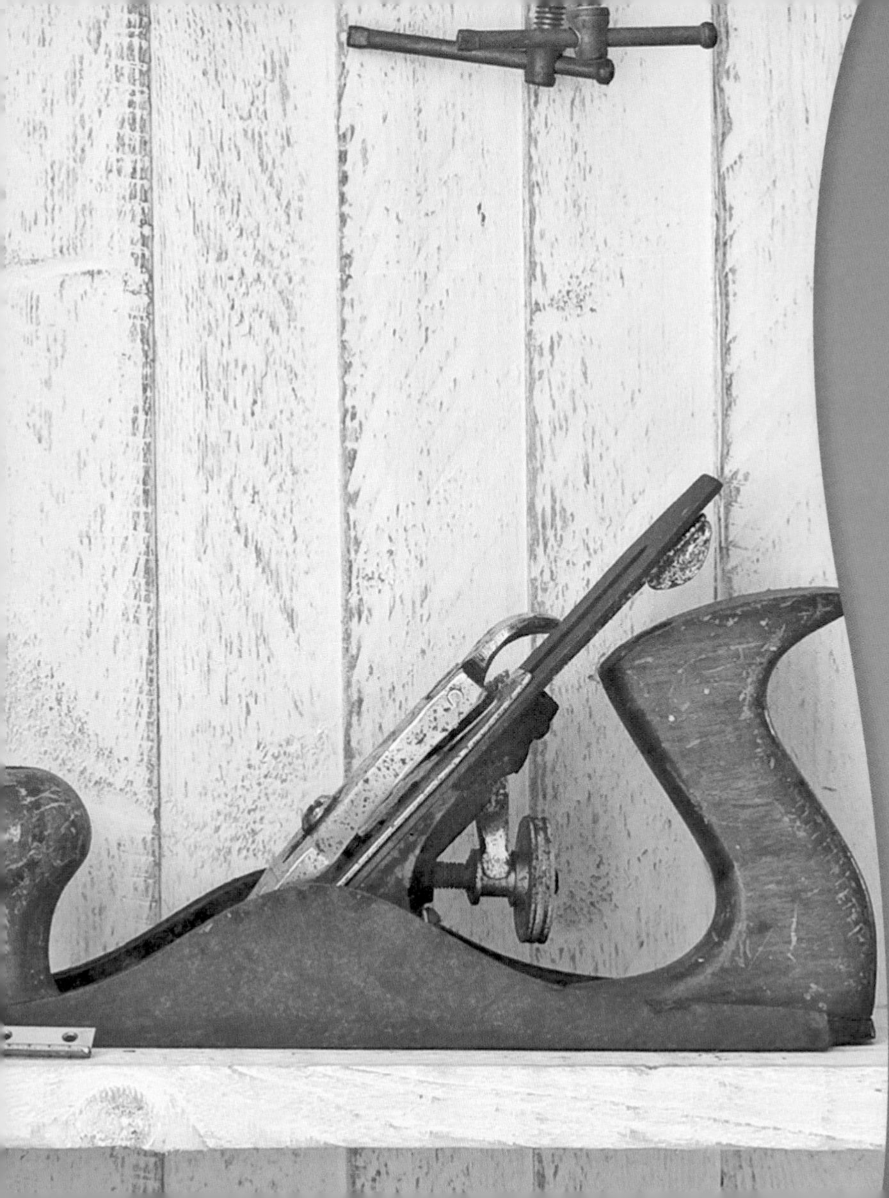

HOME IMPROVEMENTS

Do It Yourself

We now know that a lot of the chemical compounds found in many commonly used paints are harmful to our environment. However, we often forget that their use in our homes means that we are in constant touch with them. So before you reach for the synthetic chemicals, try the natural vinegar solution. Vinegar solutions for preparing wood, stone, metal and brick surfaces are cheaper, safer and more ecologically sound than many chemical preparations. Note that they are NOT recommended for use on marble.

Plaster, Wallpaper & Paint

Pliable Plaster

To keep plaster 'wet' for a little longer while you work it smooth on walls, add
2 tablespoons white vinegar to the plaster mix. This will slow down the hardening process.

Strip-ease

Stripping off old wallpaper is a messy job and can be expensive if you have to hire or buy
a steam stripper. Before you spend your money, try spraying the wallpaper until it is well
saturated with a solution of equal parts water and white vinegar, and then scrape away. If
there are tough areas, try scoring the wallpaper with a sharp blade before soaking.

Sticky Fingerprints

The acid in white vinegar cuts through grease, so it is a good cleaner for surfaces (like
staircase walls where sticky hands have made a trail) prior to painting, especially if you are
using a water-based emulsion. Paint over oily or greasy marks and they will 'float' to the
surface of your new paint, just like an oil and vinegar salad dressing that has 'separated'.

Restore Paintbrushes

Do not discard synthetic bristle brushes that have dried-on paint. Instead, soak them in
undiluted white vinegar until the paint dissolves. Brush handles usually have a hole in them:

thread a skewer or long nail through the hole and balance the brush on the edge of a jar, so the bristles are suspended in the vinegar and that way you will not get bent bristles.

Bring Brushes Back from the Dead!

If the above vinegar remedy still leaves your paintbrushes looking beyond all hope, before you consign them to the DIY graveyard try this: bring 115–230 ml/4–8 fl oz/½–1 cup white vinegar to the boil in an old saucepan and immerse the bristles in the boiling solution for 10 minutes. Then wash with warm soapy water and rinse clean.

Remove Paint Fumes

Even today's water-based and 'green' paints still have a paint odour: always make sure that when you decorate, the room is well ventilated. At the end of the job you can get rid of lingering paint smells by placing a couple of shallow bowls of neat white vinegar in the newly decorated room.

Squeaky Clean

Mildew and dust can be a problem in older properties and during renovation. Wiping the walls with undiluted white vinegar will 'kill' mildew and dampen down the dust, making removal easier. For hard-to-reach ceilings, try using a sponge mop on a pole!

Woodwork, Brickwork & Cement

Tips for Rust

Rusted saws and the blades of cutting tools can be 'sharpened' by immersing the metal in undiluted white vinegar for a couple of days. Loosen up corroded nuts and bolts in the same way, and paint vinegar on to rusted screws and hinges before you try to undo them.

Wonderful Wood

Stripped wood in all its natural beauty looks wonderful but can become dull with dirt. Taking off the dirt does not mean you have to take off a layer of wood as well – as you would with an electric sander or stripper. Before you go down the electric route, try a simpler (and less noisy) solution: mix 600 ml/1 pint/2½ cups warm water with 4 tablespoons white vinegar – or even cider vinegar – and 2 tablespoons olive oil in a sealable bottle or jar. Give it a shake and then apply to the wood with a clean cloth. Let the 'dressing' soak into the wood for a few minutes and then buff to a shine with a dry cloth.

Bright Bricks

Attractive brickwork, whether on floors, walls or fireplaces, can often be marred by white or green salt 'tide marks' called efflorescence. This occurs when the mortar or masonry units dry out and the soluble alkaline salts migrate to the surface. Washing away with water can

work for a while, but more often than not it brings more salt to the surface. To stop the problem recurring, try washing brickwork with an acid solution to neutralize the alkaline salts: 230 ml/8 fl oz/1 cup white vinegar in a bucket of warm water may just do the trick.

Painting Cement

Light grey cement may not be your favourite finish, so enliven it with colour. Painted cement, however, does have a tendency to peel after a while, but by painting the cement first with an initial coat of white vinegar and letting it dry, you will find that the paint adheres for much longer. You can also use this technique for painting galvanized metal.

Avoid Concrete and Cement Burns

We often think that only heat and acid cause burns, but strong alkalis can also cause skin blistering. It is the lime in concrete and cement mix that is highly alkaline and contact with the skin should be avoided as it can cause skin cracking and even eczema. Wash dried concrete and cement off your skin with undiluted white vinegar to neutralize the lime, then wash in warm soapy water.

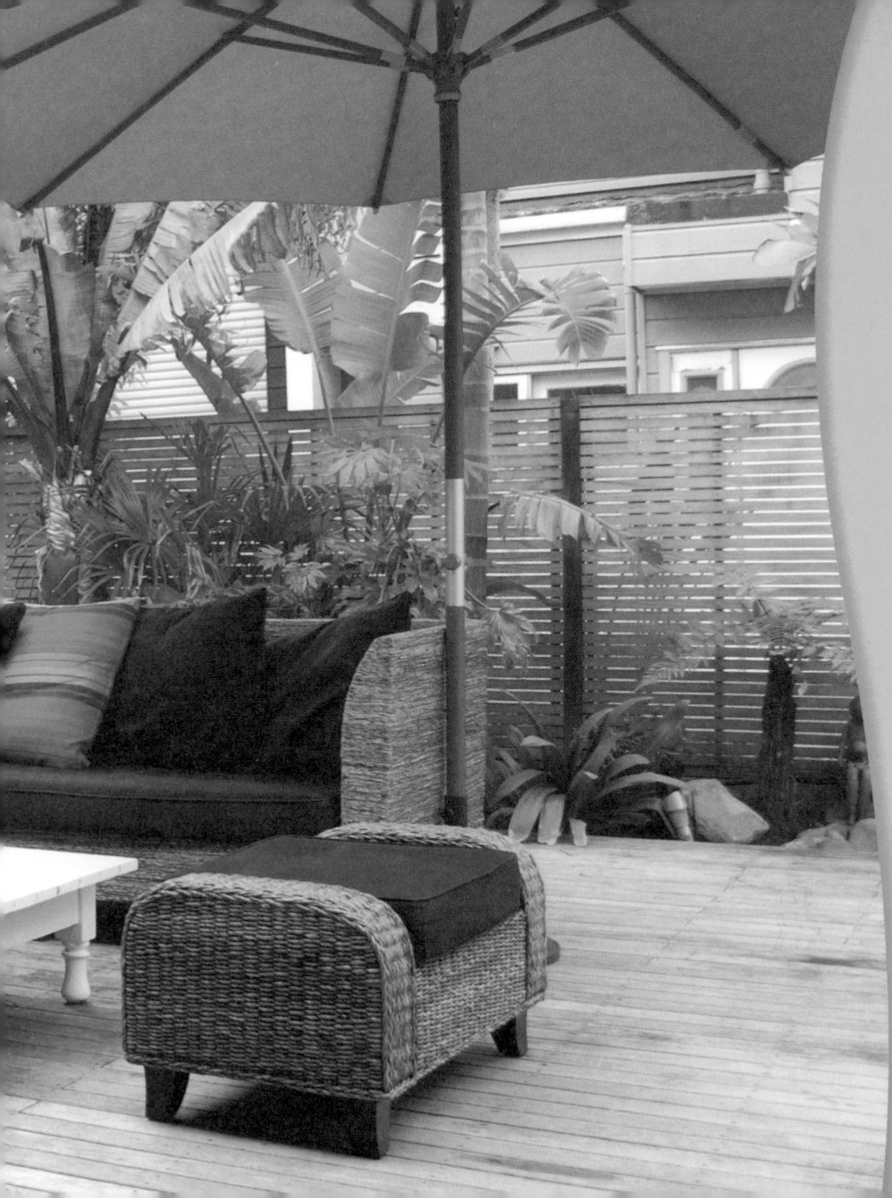

THE OUTDOORS

Gardening

Vinegar has a number of herbicidal and insecticidal uses in the garden and because it is a natural organic product you will not be harming the environment with chemicals. The vinegar that is available for household use does not normally exceed five per cent acetic acid, but stronger vinegars for use specifically as herbicides can be purchased. Solutions of over 10 per cent acidity can be 'corrosive' to skin, so make sure you handle them with care.

Improving Soil & Plant Growth

Acid or Alkaline?

Some plants like an acid soil, some like it alkaline and some – like weeds – just do not seem to care either way. Find out if your garden soil is alkaline by placing a handful of soil into a container and then pouring on 120 ml/4 fl oz/½ cup white vinegar. If the soil fizzes or bubbles, your soil is alkaline. If you have a large garden, try the test using soil from different spots to see if it is alkaline throughout.

To test for an acid soil, mix a handful of soil with 120 ml/4 fl oz/½ cup water and 2 heaped tablespoons bicarbonate of soda (baking soda). Any fizzing and bubbling this time tells you that your soil is acid. While you now know what kind of soil you have, to find out the exact pH levels you will need a simple testing kit from a garden centre.

Increase Soil Acidity

Some plants, such as azaleas, gardenias, hydrangeas and rhododendrons, thrive in acid soils. Keep an eye out for yellowing leaves on these plants as this could be signalling a lack of iron or a shift in the soil's pH level above 5.0. If you live in a hard water area, the acidity levels in your soil might be low. To bring the acidity to a comfortable level for these plants,

add 230 ml/8 fl oz/1 cup white vinegar to a each large bucket of tap water, and water once a week for three weeks. The acetic acid in the vinegar will release the iron in the soil for the plants' use.

Blooming Marvellous

With shop-bought bouquets you get a little sachet of plant food, but flowers cut from the garden are effectively put on a starvation diet! They will keep for longer if you place into your vase 2 tablespoons sugar and 2 tablespoons white vinegar for each litre/2 pints/4½ cups water. Trim the flower stems and change the 'feed' every 4–5 days.

Speed Up Sprouting

Some seeds – especially the woody seeds of plants such as gourds, passionflowers and morning glory – can be given a helping hand to germinate if you rub them gently between two sheets of fine sandpaper and then soak them overnight in a solution of 600 ml/1 pint/2½ cups warm water and 120 ml/4 fl oz/½ cup apple cider vinegar. The next morning, take the seeds out of the solution, rinse them off and plant them. Herb seeds can also be difficult to get started, and the same technique – but without the sandpaper massage – will help.

Disease, Weeds & Pests

Rust, Black Spot and Powdery Mildew

Before you buy chemicals from the garden centre, reach for the cider vinegar. Mix 1 tablespoon apple cider vinegar with 1 litre/2 pints/4½ cups water and decant into a spray bottle. Spray the vinegar solution on to the affected plants in the early morning or early evening when the temperature is relatively cool and there is no direct sunlight on the plants. Repeat until the condition is cured.

Banish Weeds

Dandelions spoiling your lawn? Banish them by spraying with undiluted white vinegar. Break off the flower head and spray the stalk and around the base of the plant in order to soak the roots. If it rains in the night, go out and spray again! The same treatment also works well for getting rid of grass on driveways and paths.

Keep Off the Grass!

There are many visitors to our gardens who are more than welcome, but there are some whom we wish would stay away. Many animals, including cats, rabbits and deer, cannot stand the smell of vinegar even when it is dry. So to stop neighbours' cats using your

borders as a lavatory, and rabbits and deer dining on your vegetable patch, soak some rags in neat white vinegar and tie them to some sticks or staves. Once a week, soak the rags in vinegar again to keep up the scent.

A 'Friendly' Fly Trap

Gnats, midges, flies and mosquitoes can all be shown the door using a simple organic trap. Take an empty plastic water or pop bottle and pour in around 120 ml/4 fl oz/½ cup apple cider vinegar, about 4 tablespoons sugar and 120 ml/4 fl oz/½ cup water. Next, cut up a banana skin into small pieces, put them in the solution and shake well. You can either tie a piece of string around the neck of the bottle and hang it from a tree branch or place it on the ground: either way, hungry flies will make a beeline for the free lunch inside, but will have great trouble exiting the neck of the bottle once there.

Give Ants their Marching Orders

An army of ants marching across your picnic table – or a child's play blanket spread on the grass – are a nuisance. Ants, however, hate the scent of vinegar, so pour or spray white vinegar around an 'exclusion zone' and they'll stay clear.

Get Rid of Mealy Bugs

Mealy bugs are one of the most common pests to be found on houseplants and in the greenhouse, where they feast on plant juices and can cause leaf drop and subsequent plant death. Look under the leaves and at the junctions with the stem: if you see these small scaly insects, then dab them with a cotton wool ball soaked in white vinegar. The vinegar will kill them – and any eggs they may have laid.

Home Exteriors

When the sun comes out, there is no better place to be than outdoors, especially if it is as comfortable and clean as indoors. Check out the home improvement section for useful tips for renovations, repair and decoration, and make sure you have your vinegar handy for the following uses.

Garden Furniture

Furniture and Decks

Wooden garden furniture and decking are very attractive additions in any outside space, but they do need regular maintenance. In warm, damp conditions mildew can be a problem, so have a handy spray bottle of full strength white vinegar to hand. The mildew will wipe off quite easily and the vinegar will keep it from coming back for a while. For large areas such as decking, use a brush and a bucket.

Shining Shades

Fabric patio umbrellas and awnings are also prone to mildew, especially if they have been stored closed through the winter. These can be cleaned and deodorized using a mix of 230 ml/8 fl oz/1 cup white vinegar, 2 tablespoons washing-up liquid and a bucket of hot water. Put your gloves on and scrub. Rinse off with clean water and open the umbrella or awning to let it air-dry – preferably in the sunshine!

Around the House

Drains

Nothing spoils a sunny day in the garden more than the smell of drains wafting in the breeze. A simple combination of vinegar and bicarbonate of soda (baking soda) is not only the most effective way to clean drains, gullies and waste water pipes, but also gentler on the pipes and your purse! Use a funnel and pour 2–3 tablespoons bicarbonate of soda (baking soda) down your sink plughole followed by 120 ml/4 fl oz/½ cup white vinegar. When the fizzing stops, flush through with hot water. Wait 5 minutes and then flush through with cold water.

Fresher Bins

Outdoor rubbish and wheelie bins should be given the same care as the one in your kitchen. When the bin has been emptied, give it a wash with a solution of 230 ml/8 fl oz/1 cup white vinegar, 2 tablespoons washing-up liquid and a bucket of hot water. Pour the solution into the bin and, using a long-handled brush or stiff broom, give it a scrub – inside and out. Rinse out with clean water to leave it clean and odour-free.

Watch the Birdie!

Messy wet droppings will disappear if you spray them with full strength white vinegar and wipe them off with a rag or paper towel that can be disposed of afterwards. When dried guano is scraped off surfaces, it turns into a fine powder that can be breathed into the lungs, so if you are cleaning up dried-on droppings, spray them well first with vinegar to damp them down. Wear a protective mask.

Automotive Care

On the Road

If your windscreen gets more blurred when it rains and you have turned the wipers on, then your wiper blades are dirty. Clean them off by running a cloth soaked in white vinegar along the entire length of each blade.

Organic De-icer

Most drivers keep a noxious can of aerosol, chemical de-icer in the car in winter and probably throw it away come spring. Save your money, and a space in the landfill site, by spraying your car windows with a solution of 3 parts white vinegar and 1 part water. You will find that it can keep frost from forming on your windows for up to two weeks.

Clean Machine

Shaking out and vacuuming car mats will remove loose dirt, but will not remove stains or smells. Deodorize car mats and remove salt deposits with a solution of equal parts white vinegar and water, and sponge it on. Leave it to sink in for a few minutes then blot up with sheets of newspaper or paper towels and let them air-dry. You can also spruce up the seat upholstery in the same way, but you will need to do this on a warm day, and leave the windows wide open so it can dry out completely.

ANIMAL CARE

Clean & Healthy

Vinegar has a vital role to play in pet care: from keeping their living, sleeping and nesting areas clean and odour-free, to keeping out unwanted pests, such as fleas and ticks, which can affect the health and wellbeing of our animals. Vinegar can also be a handy tool in the first line of defence for your pet's health.

Happy Pets

Sweet Dreams

You would not be comfortable in a dirty bed and neither will your pet. Wash their blankets as normal, but add 230 ml/8 fl oz/1 cup white vinegar to the cycle to deodorize and kill bacteria. Dogs and cats can, like their owners, suffer from sensitive skin: the vinegar will remove any remains of soap to which they may be sensitive from their bedding.

Feathered Friends

No animal enjoys eating or drinking from a dirty table, so before you fill up the bird feeder with seeds or the bird fountain with water, give them a clean. Empty out any leftovers from seed holders and immerse them in a bucket of hot water, and 230 ml/8 fl oz/1 cup white vinegar. Let them sit in the bucket until the water is cold, then rinse really well with cold water. For bird fountains, pour in a solution of 2 parts white vinegar and 1 part hot water and if possible, give the inside a good scrub. Empty out the solution and rinse really well with clean water.

Accidents Happen

House training a kitten or a puppy needs patience – and vinegar – as they will wet any previously spoiled spots because it is marked with their scent. As well as cleaning up, it is vital to remove the scent from the floor, carpet or upholstery. For carpets, rugs and upholstery, blot up as much of the stain as possible with paper towels, then pour undiluted white vinegar over the spot and blot again. Reapply the vinegar, blot and let it air-dry. For wood and vinyl floors, test an inconspicuous area with a solution of equal parts white vinegar and water to make sure it does not damage the floor's finish. If satisfactory, mop the floor and dry with a cloth or paper towel. In both instances the vinegar will remove the scent so the place will not be 'marked' again.

 CAUTION: Don't forget to test a small area on wood and vinyl floors first to check the vinegar solution causes no damage.

Dinner is Served

While dogs tend to eat their food in one sitting, cats like to graze. In either case, their dinner bowls can often hold the scent of their food, so after every feed, wash their bowls, then deodorize them with a solution of equal parts white vinegar and water, and rinse well in clean water. Remember that cats loathe the smell of vinegar, so make sure Kitty's bowl is well rinsed.

An Apple a Day…

Vinegar is acid until it enters the body, where it becomes alkaline and lines the intestines where bacteria such as *E. Coli* can no longer attach themselves. A teaspoon of apple cider vinegar added to your dogs' drinking water will keep their insides in top condition.

Tick Tactics

Fill a spray bottle with equal parts of water and white vinegar and apply directly to your pet's coat, rubbing it in well. This may take some doing with a cat because they absolutely hate the smell of vinegar, but then, it seems, so do the ticks and fleas!

Hear Kitty Kitty!

If your cat – or dog – has been scratching at their ears more than usual, a clean-out with a ball of cotton wool or a soft cloth dabbed in a dilute solution of 2 parts apple cider vinegar and 1 part water will clean them and deter ear mites.

 CAUTION: Do make a visual inspection of your pet's ears first; do not apply the vinegar, even in dilute form, to open scratches or sores.

Bites and Stings

Dab a dilute solution of apple cider vinegar and water on to bee stings and mosquito bites to relieve itching.

This is NOT a Scratching Post!

Cats absolutely hate the smell of vinegar, even after it has dried, so a little neat, white vinegar dabbed on to the proposed scratching post will thwart them!

HEALTH &
PERSONAL CARE

Apple Cider Vinegar

'An apple a day keeps the doctor away.'

This old rhyme does contain a great deal of truth: like many fruits, apples contain vitamins, minerals and other antioxidant properties which may help to reduce the risk of cancer by preventing DNA damage. Boron, the mineral that is found in apples, may retard bone loss in women after menopause and possibly help women on oestrogen replacement therapy keep the oestrogen in their bloodstream for longer.

A Multipurpose Natural Remedy

In recent years apple cider vinegar has become one of the most popular 'natural remedies' for a whole range of ailments. There have been scientific studies and medical trials supporting some of this vinegar's benefits in our diet: it can reduce cholesterol and adding 2 tablespoons (30 ml/⅛ cup) to our diet has been shown to reduce the GI (glycaemic index) of carbohydrate food. Potassium, which is found in apple cider vinegar, is vital to good health: a potassium deficiency can cause a variety of conditions including hair loss, brittle nails and sinusitis.

The vinegar also contains malic acid, which has been found to destroy micro-organisms including fungi and bacteria – which is why it has for thousands of years been used for pickling and preserving foods. Scientists now know that apple cider vinegar also inhibits the growth of gram-negative bacilli (the most well-known of which are the bacteria *E. Coli* and *Salmonella*) and because it balances the acid levels in the body, vinegar can help keep the levels of gut flora such as *Candida albicans* in the digestive tract at healthy levels: low acid levels can encourage the growth of fungal infections such as *candidiasis* (also known as 'thrush').

A Reliable Remedy?

Many of the claims for apple cider vinegar's curative properties, including 'miraculous weight-loss vinegar diets' and 'cures' for arthritis (involving drinking a mix of honey, apple cider vinegar, water and kelp 3 times a day), remain untested and unproven, but incredibly popular nonetheless and with a great deal of anecdotal support. Many advocates of apple cider vinegar 'cures' claim the acidic content of apple cider vinegar 'breaks down fat', supposedly leading to weight loss, and that the malic acid dissolves uric acid deposits that can form around joints and cause swelling and pain.

Most champions of 'vinegar treatments' recommend apple cider vinegar, but to be truly effective this must be made from fresh, organic, crushed apples that are allowed to mature naturally in wooden barrels. Such 'raw' or 'natural' apple cider vinegar can be found in most good health food shops and should have the vinegar mother clearly present as sediment in the bottom of the bottle. Distilling or pasteurizing apple cider vinegar will have not only removed the vinegar mother, but also destroyed many minerals and trace elements, including potassium, phosphorus, sulphur, magnesium, iron and copper. Also destroyed in pasteurization are malic and tartaric acids that may be beneficial in fighting toxins and inhibiting bacterial, yeast and fungal growth in the intestinal tract.

Some Drawbacks

While there are no long-term side effects to ingesting apple cider vinegar in moderation, the big drawbacks to drinking substantially larger quantities of vinegar than what you would eat in the form of salad dressing are the strong taste and the potential deterioration of dental enamel. This can give your teeth a yellowish appearance and make them much more sensitive to heat and cold. Some suggest apple cider vinegar is made more palatable by mixing it with apple juice or with bicarbonate of soda (baking soda), which neutralizes the acid to between 6.0 and 7.0 pH.

Be Prepared

If you are going to try apple cider vinegar for remedial purposes, it is also recommended that you carry out an investigation of your own by buying a pH-testing kit (you can purchase these at a local pharmacy). You can test your urine to see if you are more alkaline or acid so that you can adjust the amount of apple cider vinegar doses. You should also start with a thorough, in-depth investigation of the literature available in books and online, in tandem with a consultation with your medical practitioner.

 CAUTION: Do not attempt self-diagnosis or self-treatment: always seek qualified advice for any medical condition.

The majority of the remedies suggested in the following section use apple cider vinegar (or in some instances white vinegar) as external applications: the nearest any vinegar will get to your mouth is in the form of a mouth wash, and like any other mouthwash, you spit it out after gargling! If you are going to 'eat' vinegar, then it should be a pleasure – as part of a delicious and nutritious meal – so check out the Cookery & Recipes section.

Ailments &
Problem Conditions

Before we had medicine cabinets stuffed full of cough, cold and flu remedies, pills, powders and capsules, we would have looked to nature for remedies for our ailments. It is now acknowledged that many 'folk remedies' can be effective to varying degrees. Apple cider vinegar is one such natural product that has recently been 'rediscovered' and found to be effective in offering relief from a range of symptoms of common illnesses and infections.

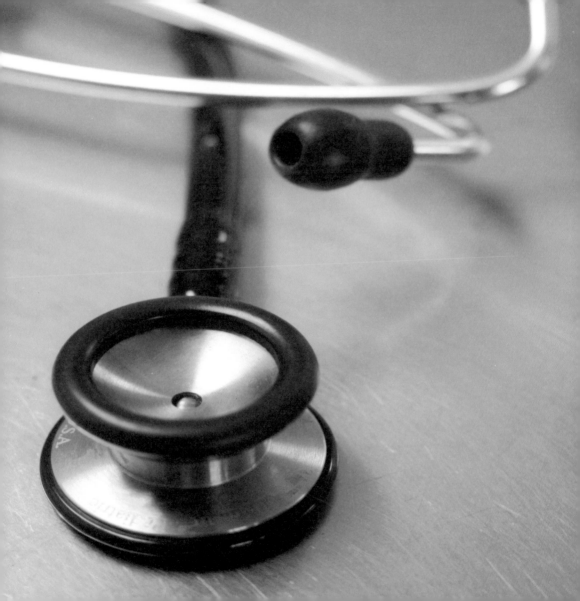

Flu & Cold Symptoms

Sinus and Chest Congestion

Congestion caused by a cold or sinus infection can be eased by a 'steam treatment'.
Put 120 ml/4 fl oz/½ cup white vinegar into a heatproof bowl and pour on some boiling
water. Breath in the steam-vapour. A towel over your head to keep the steam 'focused'
will help.

Tight Chests

An old folk remedy for chest pains and 'aching ribs' caused by a cold, flu or by coughing
is to soak a piece of brown paper in apple cider vinegar, then sprinkle one side of the wet
paper liberally with pepper. Place the paper pepper- side down against your chest and leave
it there for 20–25 minutes.

Sore Throats

A 'raw throat' from singing, talking or after a cough can be soothed by gargling with
a mix of 1 tablespoon apple cider vinegar and 1 teaspoon salt dissolved in a glass
of warm water. Use several times a day if needed.

For sore throats associated with colds and the flu, mix equal amounts cider vinegar
and honey, stir or shake until dissolved, and take a tablespoon every four hours,
letting it 'dribble' down the back of your throat.

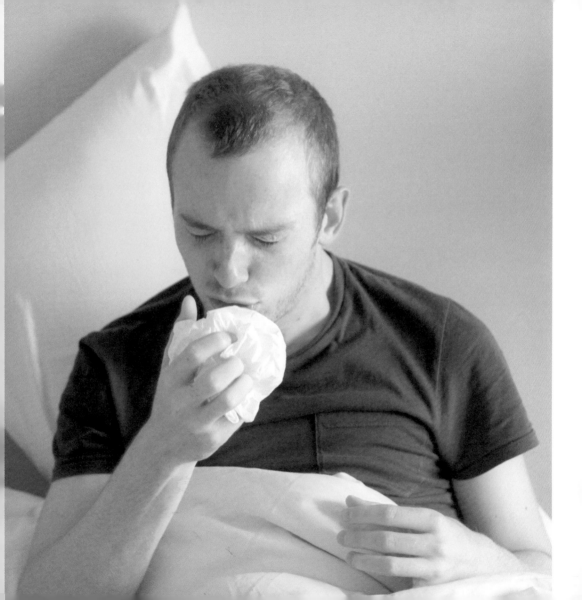

Skin Conditions

Varicose Veins

Again, this is not a cure, but is better described as 'relief': soak some 'bandages' made from clean cotton fabric in apple cider vinegar, wrap them around your legs – not too tightly – and lie down for 30 minutes with your legs comfortably supported so that your feet are above the level of your head.

Corns and Calluses

Corns are hard little 'mountains' formed by increased growth of the skin on toes and are often caused by wearing shoes that are too tight. Calluses are areas of skin that have become toughened through repeated contact or pressure and are most common on the hands.

A traditional remedy for both these problems is to saturate a slice of stale white bread in white vinegar and let it soak for 30 minutes. Then break off a piece of bread large enough to cover the corn or callused area. Keep the poultice in place with a gauze bandage and leave it on overnight.

The next morning the callused skin should have 'dissolved' and a corn should be easier to remove. Older, harder corns and calluses may need a few treatments.

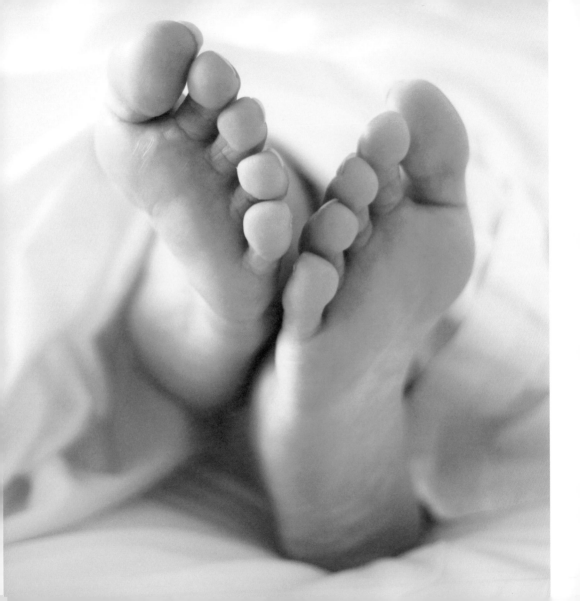

Wart Remover

Warts are caused by a viral infection, specifically by the *human papillomavirus*. One folk remedy is to soak the wart for 20 minutes each day in white vinegar, followed by a gentle rub with an emery board, until it disappears. You could also apply a vinegar-soaked cotton pad and bandage this to the wart.

Cold Sores

Cold sores are caused by a viral infection (known as *herpes simplex* type 1) and are small, painful fluid-filled blisters on the mouth or round the nostrils. Once you have had a cold sore, the virus lies dormant in the nerves or skin around the original site until something – a cold, the flu, stress or generally being 'run-down' – causes another outbreak. You can sooth the pain and swelling, and perhaps 'disinfect' the sore by dabbing with a cotton wool ball soaked in apple cider vinegar 3 times a day.

Pimples and Spots

Apple cider vinegar can help clear the complexion by balancing the skin's pH level and absorbing excess oil from the skin. A dilute solution of 1 part apple cider vinegar and 3 to 4 parts water applied 3 times a day to the skin and left there for 10 minutes or so before rinsing off will help clear the complexion.

Athlete's Foot

Medically known as *Tinea Pedis*, you do not have to be an athlete to suffer from this fungal infection. It commonly affects the feet but it can be spread – on bath towels – to other parts

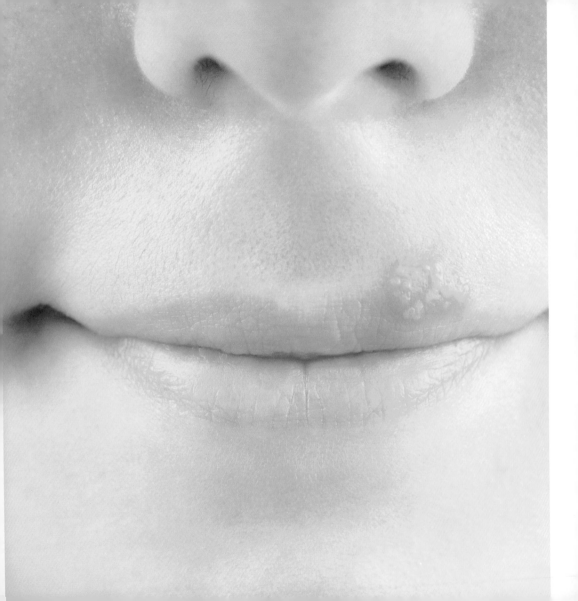

of the body (especially the crotch) because the fungus needs a nice warm, moist and dark place to thrive!

Keeping feet (and other 'bits') dry, and going barefoot whenever possible, are recommended, but to get rid of the fungus itself (and ease the itching), rinse your feet 3 or 4 times a day with undiluted apple cider vinegar. To guard against re-infection, soak your socks (and jocks!) in a solution of 1 part white vinegar and 4 parts warm water for 30 minutes before laundering.

Sunburn

Cool sunburn by gently dabbing the affected area with a cotton ball or a soft cloth saturated with white or cider vinegar. This treatment is most effective if you can treat the burn before it starts to sting.

Nappy Rash

You do not actually need to be a baby to get nappy (diaper) rash, although it is babies who are usually associated with this redness and scaling. It is caused by cloth that has been rubbing against the skin for too long, fitting too tightly or been left on for too long. Irritation is also very often caused by the soap residues in cloth nappies and underwear, so rinse these in a mild solution of water and white vinegar – about 120 ml/4 fl oz/½ cup to 2.3 litres/4 pints/9⅔ cups of water to neutralize the alkaline of the soap and balance the pH level.

Itchy Skin

The temptation when you get an itch is to scratch, and so break the skin. Insect bites are a common cause of itchiness but a paste made from apple cider vinegar and cornflour

(cornstarch) will help reduce the urge to scratch. For overall dry and itchy skin, 2 tablespoons vinegar added to your bath water will help soothe the itch and, being more relaxed, it should also make you less 'antsy'.

Mosquito Bites

The whining buzz of a mosquito in your ear is in fact the love song of the male mosquito and while the noise may drive you mad, you can take heart in knowing that he will not bite. It is the female mosquito who is the silent bloodsucker and leaves behind her calling card of a nasty, incessant itch, which if scratched too hard can break the skin and lead to an open wound and infection.

Alleviate the itch with apple cider vinegar. Not only will it calm the itch, but many claim that the scent of vinegar keeps the mosquitoes from coming back for a second helping.

'Vinegar for Vasp' Stings

Use the simple mnemonic above to remind you of how to treat a wasp sting; their sting is alkaline so is neutralized by the acetic acid in vinegar. Remove the stinger by scraping the blunt edge of a butter knife in the opposite direction to the point of entry into the skin. A ball of cotton wool soaked in apple cider vinegar and applied to the stung area should reduce the pain and inflammation.

 CAUTION: If you have any redness and/or swelling 24 hours after being stung you may have an infection, so consult a doctor. If you have had a severe reaction to a sting or bite in the past, you should consult your doctor about the need for an emergency syringe of epinephrine to be carried at all times outdoors.

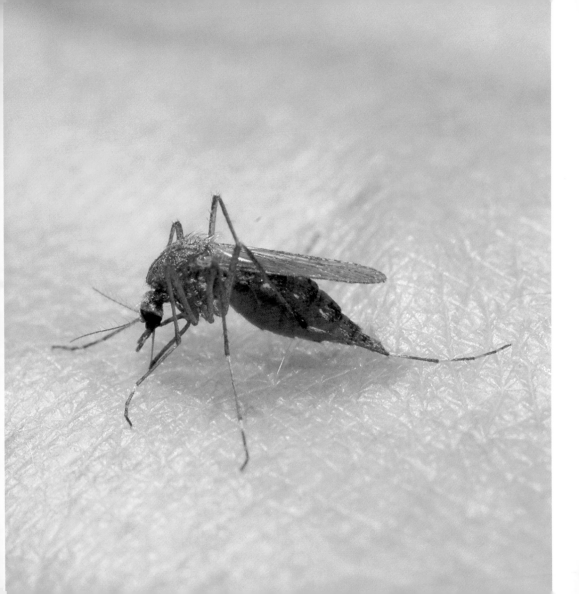

Aches & Discomfort

Sore Muscles

After a workout in the gym or a long day's work, treat your aching muscles to a soak in a pleasantly hot tub with 120 ml/4 fl oz/½ cup cider vinegar added to the bath water.

Better Digestion

The acetic acid in vinegar is said to help prevent the naturally important hydrochloric acid, which is vital in the process of food digestion, from leaving the stomach too quickly. Food is digested more completely with less 'reflux', belching, 'wind' or indigestion pains. Instead of a chemical indigestion remedy, 1 teaspoon apple cider vinegar mixed with 1–2 teaspoons honey in a glass of water may do the job just as well.

Hiccups

Medically known as *singultis*, hiccups are caused by a sudden spasm of the diaphragm which causes air to be rushed into the lungs, leading the epiglottis to close – which is the 'hic' sound in the hiccups.

A bout of hiccups normally resolves itself, but an old remedy that claims to 'cure' hiccups is a teaspoon of apple cider vinegar. Rather than any medicinal properties in the vinegar effecting a 'cure', it is more likely to be the sour taste – making you screw your face up and hold your breath – that does the trick!

Improving Appearance

The astringent and toning qualities of vinegar – particularly apple cider vinegar – have for centuries been used as part of women's – and men's – beauty regimes. Vinegar is much more astringent than ice and will reduce inflammation, redness, bruising and swelling in about half the time.

Skin

 CAUTION: Do not apply vinegar – even in dilute solutions – to broken skin (grazes, scratches and cuts) and if you have sensitive skin, rinse off immediately. The acidic nature of vinegar means that you should not apply it to your eyes.

Age Spots

Age spots, caused by hormonal changes, and sun spots, due to overexposure to the sun, can often be successfully remedied by dabbing with full-strength apple cider vinegar applied with a cotton wool ball for about 10 minutes twice a day.

Often the spots will fade in a few weeks, but if they worry you or you notice any significant increase in size or darkness, consult your medical practitioner.

Broken Veins and Bruises

As a gentle astringent, apple cider vinegar is a useful treatment for those tiny, but unsightly, broken veins that can often appear on the surface of skin. Dab on undiluted apple cider vinegar to speed the repair and reduce redness. Bruises can also be treated in the same way.

Skin Toner

The use of vinegar as a skin toner dates back to the ancient Egyptians. After cleaning your face, add 1 tablespoon apple cider vinegar to a basin of cool water and rinse. You will notice any residual grease from make-up and make-up removers disappear and your skin is cooled, toned and feels a little 'tighter'. Take care not to get the solution in your eyes: if you accidentally splash it in your eyes, rinse out with cold water.

Soft Skin

Apple cider vinegar added to a soaking bath – or even vinegar-soaked 'bandages' wrapped around knees and elbows and left on overnight – are the 'lazy way' to deal with rough or hard skin. In the morning, bathe as usual and gently rub the dry areas with a pumice stone in small circular motions to remove dead skin.

Pleasant Pits

Many commercial antiperspirants contain chemicals and minerals such as zinc to stop you sweating. Many 'natural' deodorants do not stop you sweating but instead mask any body odour with a scent. The antibacterial and deodorizing properties of vinegar can be harnessed by splashing or dabbing a little white vinegar under each arm. You can even steep a few leaves of herbs – sage is good – in the vinegar if you want a 'scented' lotion (sage is also 'cooling' on the skin). As well as combating odour, the vinegar will not make those white marks on your clothes that many ordinary antiperspirants leave behind.

 CAUTION: Remember – do not apply vinegar to broken skin (or after hair removal by shaving) as it will sting!

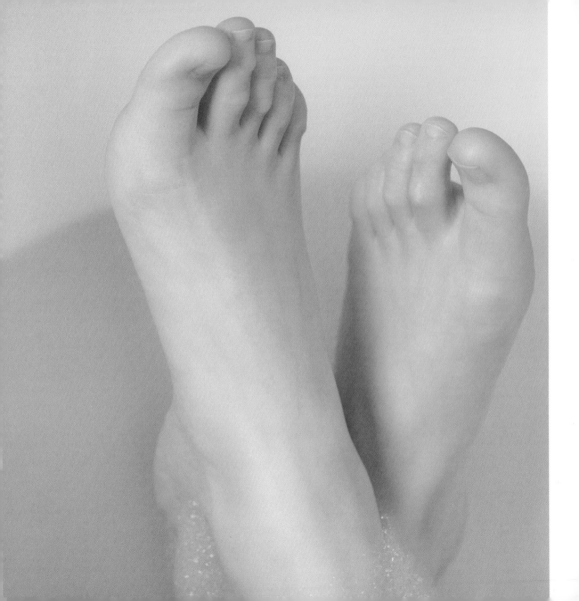

Hair

Dandruff

Rinsing your hair with a warm water solution containing apple cider vinegar can help alleviate dandruff. Try a solution with equal measures water and vinegar for an overall 'rinse', or treat a problem area by applying a tablespoon of apple cider vinegar on to the hair and massage gently with your fingertips. Wait a few minutes, then wash as normal and rinse well in warm water. The acetic acid in the vinegar kills the fungus *Malassezia furfur* and restores the pH balance of the scalp.

Remember that too-hot water will make the texture of your hair 'dry', while rubbing your scalp too much will stimulate the sebaceous glands to release their oils, resulting in greasy hair.

Blonde Protection

Blonde hair – whether natural or by design – can need extra protection, especially if you swim in chlorinated pools. The chlorine keeps the water safe but it can give blonde hair a greenish tinge, so to protect it, rub apple cider vinegar into your hair and let it set for 15 minutes or so before taking the plunge.

Hair Conditioner

Bring the life back into limp or damaged hair with a nourishing hair conditioner.
Whip together 1 teaspoon apple cider vinegar with 2 tablespoons almond or olive
oil and 3 egg whites.

Gently massage the mix into your hair and then cover with a shower cap – or plastic
wrap – for 30 minutes. Rinse with warm – not hot – water, unless you want scrambled
egg whites cooked in your hair! Then shampoo and wash as normal.

Nitty-gritty

Head lice, known scientifically as *Pediculosis capitis*, are commonly associated with
schoolchildren, but adults can get them too. Contrary to popular opinion, which implies that
those who get head lice have dirty hair, head lice adore squeaky clean and preferably fine,
straight hair. The lice are keen travellers looking for 'human hotels' and are most often
spread by being transferred between clothing.

While head lice themselves do not transmit disease, unless treated, their itchy infestation
can be embarrassing and make life a misery. The wingless 1 mm lice feed on the scalp
and lay their eggs – the nits – which are each 'glued' to a single hair close to the scalp.

An over-the-counter preparation will kill the lice, but after shampooing, an extra treatment
rinsing an infected head with white vinegar will dissolve the 'glue' holding the eggs to the
hair, which should then be combed out using a very fine-toothed comb. The treatment will
need to be repeated every 4–5 days until the hair is clear of infestation.

Nails

Soften Cuticles

A manicure or pedicure requires attention not only to the nails but to the cuticles as well. Soften cuticles by soaking your fingers and toes in white vinegar for 5 minutes.

Longer Lasting Nail Polish

Nail polish lasts longer if you dampen the nails first with a cotton wool ball soaked in apple cider or white vinegar. Let the nails dry briefly and then apply your favourite shade.

Healthy Toenails

While you are pampering your feet, take a moment or two to inspect the condition of your toenails: modern synthetic hosiery, training shoes and wearing closed shoes for days on end where toes are in slightly damp, dark and airless conditions can provide the ideal home for fungal infections which often go unnoticed until they become a real problem.

Give foot fungus the boot with regular footbaths made of 1 part vinegar (any type) to 2 parts warm water. Sit back, relax and soak away aching feet safe in the knowledge that they will be deodorized, softened and healthy – perfect for going shoe shopping!

COOKERY & RECIPES

The Basics

The wonders of vinegar? Hannibal knew, Hippocrates certainly did and, as we have seen, so did Cleopatra. Records show it was as early as 3000 BC that vinegar was produced commercially and used in every facet of life – as an effective remedy for many ailments, for all kinds of cleaning, for veterinary purposes, as well as being extremely useful both in agriculture and horticulture. But let's not forget its invaluable use in food preparation and flavouring...

Make Vinegar from Scratch

The Mother

First you need the 'vinegar mother': place 2 tablespoons vinegar and half a bottle of wine or cider in a bowl and leave for 2 weeks uncovered in a sunny position. The skin that forms is the 'acetobacter' or 'mother'. This is your starter.

Take Time

Skim off the 'mother' and place it with more of the same wine or cider originally used into a clean bowl, ensuring that the 'mother' remains on top. Cover with muslin or other porous material that will allow plenty of oxygen through while protecting the liquid from insects. Leave in a warm place for 1 month or longer, until you are happy with the taste.

Now You Have Your Vinegar

Strain off the vinegar intro a sterile bottle and cork. Add more alcohol to the 'mother' in order to start again – the 'mother' lasts indefinitely, as long as fresh alcohol is 'fed' to it.

Culinary Tips

Perfect Poached Eggs

Add a few drops of distilled white or white wine vinegar to the water when poaching eggs; this will help to keep the white intact.

No More Cracks

Add 2 teaspoons vinegar to the water when boiling eggs to prevent them from cracking.

Tender Meat

Add 1 tablespoon of a vinegar, such as red wine or cider vinegar, to stews and casseroles to help tenderize the meat. When marinating meat, add 1 tablespoon vinegar to the marinade, which again will help to tenderize.

Kill Germs

Lightly wiping raw meat with a little vinegar will help to eradicate bacteria.

Keep Food Longer

Vinegar acts as a preserver – olives when covered in white wine vinegar and kept covered in the refrigerator will keep indefinitely.

Cut Through Grease

When eating fried food, such as chips,
sprinkle with a few drops of vinegar to remove
the greasy taste and feel to the mouth. Some
will argue that it helps your body 'break down
the fat' too! (See page 140.)

Flavour Enhancer

Add a zing to boring bland dishes by adding
2–3 teaspoons vinegar. Try balsamic and look
for the different balsamic flavours.

De-glazing the Pan

Add 1–2 tablespoons vinegar to de-glaze a
frying pan or roasting tin. (Adding liquid to the
dried and caramelized meat juices in the pan
after cooking meat provides a delicious jus
or gravy.)

Clean Pudding Pans

When steaming a pudding, add a few drops of
vinegar to the water in the bottom of the pan.
This will keep the pan clean.

Flavoured Vinegars

Recently, there has been an explosion of flavoured vinegars available on the market, especially with balsamic vinegar, of which there are now varieties featuring herbs and flowers. Although considered a wine vinegar, it is actually made from grape pressings that have never been permitted to ferment into wine. Its rich, smooth depth of flavour is imparted to the food when used in cooking.

Rosemary Vinegar

Makes 600 ml/1 pint/2½ cups

450 g/1 lb fresh rosemary sprigs, rinsed

600 ml/1 pint/2½ cups white wine or cider vinegar

This recipe can be used with a variety of herbs – try tarragon, thyme, bay and oregano. The more delicate herbs such as basil, dill, mint and coriander will need their leaves bruising slightly. Avoid using dried herbs or spices as these could make the vinegar cloudy. For maximum flavour, if you grow your own rosemary, pick it first thing in the morning after the dew has dried and before it gets hot. The essential oils are released when it is around 30°C/85°F.

1 Discard the woody stems from the rosemary and place half in a glass bowl. Pour over the vinegar, stir, cover lightly and leave in a cool place for 7 days, stirring occasionally.

2 Strain, discarding the rosemary. Repeat with the remaining rosemary and pour the strained vinegar over. Cover lightly, stir occasionally and then leave for a further 7 days.

3 Pour through a fine sieve into sterilized bottles. Add 2–3 rinsed fresh rosemary sprigs and screw down tightly. Store in a dark place.

Rose Vinegar

Makes approx.
600 ml/1 pint/2½ cups

350 g/12 oz/1½ cups
rose petals

approx. 300ml/½ pint/1¼ cups
white wine vinegar

This is a delicately flavoured vinegar that is perfect to use as a dressing on salads or vegetables. Make sure that you use rose petals that have a perfume. Petals from other edible flowers can be used in this way too: try chrysanthemums, nasturtiums, marigolds or sweet peas.

1 Lightly rinse and dry the petals, ensuring that there are no insects or bugs.

2 Place in a sterilized 300 ml/½ pint/1¼ cup glass jar with a screw lid. Do not pack down too firmly.

3 Cover with white wine vinegar, seal and leave in a sunny place for at least 1 month before using.

Spiced Vinegar

Makes 700 ml/1¼ pints/3 cups

6 tsp peppercorns
3 tsp mustard seeds
2 tsp allspice

1 blade mace
1 large cinnamon stick, bruised
4 fresh bay leaves
1 small piece root ginger,
   chopped

1 tbsp salt
700 ml/1¼ pints/3 cups
   malt vinegar

This is perfect if wishing to make your own pickles and chutneys. Again, you can vary the spices used according to personal preference. White distilled vinegar is often used as it gives a sharper tang, but white wine, red whine or malt vinegar is fine to use too.

1 Tie all the spices into a piece of muslin and place in a non-reactive saucepan.

2 Add 230 ml/8 fl oz/1 cup of the vinegar and bring to the boil. Boil for 3 minutes.

3 Add the remaining vinegar and boil for a further 3 minutes.

4 Remove from the heat and leave covered for at least 24 hours. Strain into sterilized bottles and screw down.

Dressings, Sauces & Chutneys

Dressings and sauces jazz up dishes brilliantly.

They should be quick and easy to make, use the simplest ingredients

and yet give an explosion of taste. It is also really easy to make delicious,

exotic and fantastic chutneys, ceviches and pickles to liven up all

hot or cold dishes. Vinegar is key to all these recipes.

Classic Vinaigrette

**Makes 145 ml/
5 fl oz/⅔ cup**

4 tbsp olive oil

1½ tbsp white wine vinegar

1–2 tsp sugar, or to taste

freshly ground black pepper
to taste

freshly milled rock salt to taste

1 tsp mustard powder

1 tsp caster/superfine sugar, or
to taste

This dressing is used universally and can vary immensely according to local tastes
and ingredients.

1 Place all the ingredients into a screw-top jar
and shake until thoroughly blended.

2 Adjust seasoning and sweetness to taste.
Use as required.

Store in a cool cupboard, but not in the refrigerator,
as this will make the olive oil go cloudy. If preferred,
replace the sugar with 1 teaspoon clear honey;
replace 1 tablespoon of the vinegar with either
balsamic vinegar, red wine vinegar or a herb vinegar;
or add 1–2 teaspoons crushed garlic or finely
chopped chilli. You can also add 1 tablespoon
finely chopped fresh herbs.

Hollandaise Sauce

Makes 145 ml/
5 fl oz/⅔ cup

2 tbsp tarragon or white
   wine vinegar

1 tbsp water

2 fresh medium/large
   egg yolks

75–100g/3–3½ oz/6–7 tbsp
   unsalted butter, cut
   into small dice

freshly milled rock salt and
   freshly ground black pepper

This is a true classic and is perfect for serving with fish, eggs and vegetables.

1 Boil the vinegar and water together until reduced by about
   half. Leave to cool.

2 Place the egg yolks in a small bowl and stir in the cooled
   vinegar solution.

3 Place the bowl over a pan of gently simmering water and
   heat, whisking until the mixture thickens.

4 Gradually whisk in the butter, whisking well after each addition. Continue until all
   the butter has been added.

5 Season to taste and if the sauce is too sharp, add a little more butter, or if too thick,
   add a little hot water.

Crème Fraîche Dressing

2 tsp Dijon mustard, or to taste

85 ml/3 fl oz/⅓ cup
crème fraîche

freshly ground black pepper

4 tbsp extra virgin olive oil

2 tbsp champagne or white
wine vinegar

This makes a delicious change from mayonnaise.

1   Place the mustard, crème fraîche, pepper, olive oil
    and vinegar in a screw-top jar and shake until blended.
    Use as required.

    If liked, fromage frais can be used in place
    of the crème fraîche.

BBQ Sauce

Makes about 145 ml/
5 fl oz/⅔ cup

50 g/2 oz/4 tbsp butter

1 large onion, peeled and
finely chopped

1 tsp tomato paste

2 tbsp herb vinegar such as
tarragon or rosemary

1–2 tbsp soft brown sugar,
or to taste

2 tsp dry mustard powder

2 tbsp Worcestershire sauce

145 ml/5 fl oz/⅔ cup water

1 Melt the butter in a saucepan and gently fry the onion for 4 minutes, stirring frequently.

2 Add the tomato paste and continue to fry for 2 minutes.

3 Blend the remaining ingredients together, add to the pan and bring to the boil.

4 Reduce the heat and simmer for 8–10 minutes or until a thick sauce consistency
is reached. Use as required.

Mint Sauce

Makes 85 ml/
3 fl oz/⅓ cup

25 g/1 oz/2 tbsp fresh
  mint sprigs

2 tsp caster/superfine sugar
  or clear honey

2 tbsp boiling water

2 tbsp white wine vinegar

1 tbsp balsamic vinegar

Ideal to serve with all lamb dishes. Try adding a spoonful or two to a lamb casserole or stew.

1 Strip off the mint leaves from the stalks and chop finely. Place in a small bowl and add the sugar or honey.

2 Pour over the boiling water, stir well and then leave for 5 minutes.

3 Add both vinegars, stir well and pour into a sauce boat. Leave for 1 hour before using.

Salmon Ceviche

Serves 4

350 g/¾ lb fresh salmon
   fillet, skinned
145 ml/5 fl oz/⅔ cup
   lime juice

2 tbsp sherry vinegar
1 tbsp balsamic vinegar
1 bag salad leaves
100 g/4 oz/¾ cup halved
   cherry tomatoes

small piece cucumber,
   sliced

The vinegar in this recipe marinates the salmon in place of cooking it. Other very fresh fish can be used in this manner – try cod, haddock, monkfish or trout.

1 Lightly rinse the salmon and cut into small cubes; place in a bowl.

2 Blend the lime juice with the vinegars and pour over the salmon. Cover and leave in the refrigerator to marinate for at least 12 hours or overnight if possible. Stir occasionally.

3 When ready to serve, arrange the salad leaves on four individual plates and add the tomatoes and cucumber on top. Drain the salmon, place on top of the salad and serve.

Mango, Apricot & Cranberry Chutney

Makes about 1.5 kg/3 lb

8 ripe but still firm mangos

450 g/1 lb/c. 5 fresh apricots

225 g/8 oz/2¼ cups
  fresh cranberries

½ tsp salt

450 g/1 lb/3 cups peeled and
  chopped onions

2–4 green chillies, seeded
  and chopped

3 garlic cloves, peeled
  and chopped

7.5 cm/3 inch piece root
  ginger, grated

460 ml/¾ pint/2 cups cider vinegar

550 g/1 lb 4 oz/2½ cups soft
  light brown sugar

juice of 1 large lemon

You can vary the flavour of this chutney by using different fruits
and vinegars. Simply use this as your basic recipe.

1 Peel the mangos, discard the stones and roughly chop the flesh.
   Place in a non-reactive preserving or large pan. Stone the apricots,
   chop roughly and add to the pans together with all the remaining
   ingredients.

2 Place over a gentle heat and heat until the sugar has completely
   dissolved, stirring occasionally.

3 Bring to the boil, reduce the heat to a simmer and cook for 1 hour or
   until really soft and a thick consistency is reached. Taste and adjust sweetness then put
   in clean sterilized jars. When cold, cover, label and store in a cool dark place for
   1 month before using.

Mixed Pickles

**Makes 900 g/2 lb/
4 cups**

900 g/2 lbs/4 cups mixed
vegetables such as

cauliflower, broccoli, shallots,
cucumber, French/green
beans, courgette/zucchini
and carrots

3 tbsp salt

1 litre/2 pints/4½ cups spiced
vinegar (see page 186)

All manner of vegetables can be used for this pickle. It is ideal for pickling excess
vegetables when they are in season and there is a glut.

1 If using cauliflower or broccoli, break into small florets, peel the shallots and cucumber,
and discard the seeds. Trim the beans and wash thoroughly, then chop into small
pieces. Peel the courgette/zucchini and cut into small chunks. Peel the carrots and dice.

2 Dissolve the salt in 1 litre/2 pints/4½ cups water. Place all the
vegetables in a large bowl and pour over the brine. Leave overnight.

3 Next day, rinse thoroughly at least 3–4 times to remove
any excess salt, then drain and dry on clean cloths. Pack into
sterilized jars and cover with the vinegar. Cover with non-reactive
lids. Label and store in a cool dark place.

Starters, Salads & Side Dishes

If not used carefully, vinegar can swamp the flavour of some foods. This applies particularly to starters and salads, which often consist of raw ingredients with a mild delicate flavour that is easily destroyed. One good way to overcome this is to use in a dressing or sauce a vinegar that has been 'aged' and, of course, to use the correct amount. A mature mellow flavour from an 'aged' vinegar such as balsamic will enhance rather than destroy the dish.

Beetroot & Potato Medley

Serves 4

350 g/12 oz/2 cups raw
   baby beetroot
½ tsp sunflower oil
5–6 (225 g/¾ lb) new potatoes

½ cucumber, peeled
3 tbsp white wine vinegar
150 ml/5 fl oz/½ cup
   natural yogurt

salt and freshly ground
   black pepper
fresh salad leaves
1 tbsp freshly snipped chives,
   to garnish

1　Preheat the oven to 180°C/350°F/Gas Mark 4. Scrub the beetroot thoroughly and place
   on a baking tray.

2　Brush the beetroot with a little oil and cook for 1½ hours or until a skewer is easily
   insertable into the beetroot. Allow to cool a little, then remove the skins.

3　Cook the potatoes in boiling water for about 10 minutes. Rinse in cold water and drain.
   Reserve the potatoes until cool. Dice evenly.

4　Cut the cucumber into cubes and place in a mixing bowl. Chop the beetroot
   into small cubes and add to the bowl with the reserved potatoes. Gently mix the
   vegetables together.

5　Mix together the vinegar and yogurt and season to taste with a little salt and pepper.
   Pour over the vegetables and combine gently.

6　Arrange on a bed of salad leaves, garnish with the snipped chives and serve.

French Onion Tart

Serves 4
Quick flaky pastry:
125 g/4 oz/½ cup butter
175 g/6 oz/1¾ cups plain/
   all-purpose flour
pinch of salt

For the filling:
2 tbsp olive oil
4 large onions, peeled and
   thinly sliced
2 tbsp light brown sugar
3 tbsp white wine vinegar

a little beaten egg or milk
175 g/6 oz/1½ cups grated
   Cheddar cheese
salt and freshly ground
   black pepper

1 Preheat the oven to 200°C/400°F/Gas Mark 6. Place the butter in the freezer for 30
   minutes. Sift the flour and salt into a large bowl. Remove the butter from the freezer
   and grate using the coarse side of a grater, dipping the butter in the flour every now and
   again as it makes it easier to grate. Mix the butter into the flour, using a knife, making
   sure all the butter is coated thoroughly with flour. Add 2 tablespoons cold water and
   continue to mix, bringing the mixture together. Use your hands to complete the mixing.
   Add a little more water, if needed to leave a clean bowl. Place the pastry in a polythene
   bag and chill in the refrigerator for 30 minutes.

2 Heat the oil in a large frying pan, then fry the onions for 10 minutes, stirring occasionally
   until softened. Stir in the sugar and white wine vinegar. Increase the heat and stir
   frequently, for another 4–5 minutes until the onions turn a deep caramel colour. Cook for
   another 5 minutes, then reserve to cool.

3 On a lightly floured surface, roll out the pastry to a 35.5 cm/14-inch circle. Wrap over a
   rolling pin and transfer to a baking sheet. Sprinkle over half the cheese, leaving a 5 cm/
   2-inch border, then spoon over the onions. Fold the uncovered pastry edges over to form
   a rim and brush it with beaten egg or milk. Season to taste with salt and pepper. Sprinkle
   over the remaining cheese and bake for 20–25 minutes. Serve immediately.

Panzanella

Serves 4

250 g/9 oz/1 loaf
 (9 thick slices) day-old
 Italian-style bread
1 tbsp red wine vinegar
4 tbsp olive oil
1 tsp lemon juice

1 small garlic clove, peeled
 and finely chopped
1 red onion, peeled and
 finely sliced
1 cucumber, peeled if preferred
2 medium ripe tomatoes,
 deseeded

150 g/5 oz/¾ cup pitted
 black olives
about 20 basil leaves, coarsely
 torn or left whole if small
sea salt and freshly ground
 black pepper

1 Cut the bread into thick slices, leaving the crusts on. Add 1 teaspoon red wine vinegar to a jug of iced water, put the slices of bread in a bowl and pour over the water. Make sure the bread is covered completely. Leave to soak for 3–4 minutes until just soft.

2 Remove the soaked bread from the water and squeeze it gently, first with your hands and then in a clean tea towel to remove any excess water. Put the bread on a plate, cover with clingfilm and chill in the refrigerator for about 1 hour.

3 Meanwhile, whisk together the olive oil, the remaining red wine vinegar and lemon juice in a large serving bowl. Add the garlic and onion and stir to coat well.

4 Halve the cucumber and remove the seeds. Chop both the cucumber and tomatoes into 1 cm/½-inch dice. Add to the garlic and onions with the olives. Tear the bread into bite-size chunks and add to the bowl with the fresh basil leaves. Toss together to mix and serve immediately, with a grinding of sea salt and black pepper.

Warm Chicken & Potato Salad with Peas & Mint

Serves 4–6

9–12 (450 g/1 lb) new potatoes,
  peeled or scrubbed and cut
  into bite-size pieces
salt and freshly ground
  black pepper
2 tbsp cider vinegar
175 g/6 oz/1½ cups frozen
  garden peas, thawed

1 small ripe avocado
4 cooked chicken breasts,
  about 450 g/1 lb in weight,
  skinned and diced
2 tbsp freshly chopped mint
2 heads small lettuce
fresh mint sprigs, to garnish

For the dressing:

2 tbsp raspberry or sherry vinegar
2 tsp Dijon mustard
1 tsp clear honey
50 ml/2 fl oz/¼ cup
  sunflower oil
50 ml/2 fl oz/¼ cup
  extra virgin olive oil

1 Cook the potatoes in lightly salted boiling water for 15 minutes, or until just tender; do not overcook. Rinse under cold running water to cool slightly, then drain and turn into a large bowl. Sprinkle with the cider vinegar and toss gently.

2 Run the peas under hot water to ensure that they are thawed, pat dry with absorbent kitchen paper and add to the potatoes.

3 Cut the avocado in half lengthways and remove the stone. Peel and cut the avocado into cubes, and add to the potatoes and peas. Add the chicken and stir together lightly.

4 To make the dressing, place all the ingredients in a screw-top jar, with a little salt and pepper, and shake well to mix; add a little more oil if the flavour is too sharp. Pour over the salad and toss gently to coat. Sprinkle in half the mint and stir lightly.

5 Separate the lettuce leaves and spread on to a large shallow serving plate. Spoon the salad on top and sprinkle with the remaining mint. Garnish with mint sprigs and serve.

Main Courses

The use of vinegar in main meals goes a step further than in dressings and starters. Here vinegar often plays a dual role, especially in the cooking of meat. To tenderize meat, it is marinated in a mixture of vinegar, oil and spices or herbs. Vinegar added during cooking intensifies the depth of flavour. It can also be added at the very end to give a delicious glaze to the finished dish. In the following recipes all manner of vinegars have been used from cider to rice to balsamic.

Seared Duck with Pickled Plums

Serves 4

4 small skinless, boneless
　duck breasts
2 garlic cloves, peeled
　and crushed
1 tsp hot chilli sauce
2 tsp clear honey
2 tsp dark brown sugar

juice of 1 lime
1 tbsp dark soy sauce
6 large plums, halved and
　stones removed
50 g/2 oz/4 tbsp caster sugar
50 ml/2 fl oz/¼ cup white
　wine vinegar
¼ tsp dried chilli flakes

¼ tsp ground cinnamon
1 tbsp sunflower oil
145 ml/5 fl oz/⅔ cup
　chicken stock
2 tbsp oyster sauce
sprigs of fresh flat leaf parsley,
　to garnish
freshly cooked noodles, to serve

1　Cut a few deep slashes in each duck breast and place in a shallow dish. Mix together the garlic, chilli sauce, honey, brown sugar, lime juice and soy sauce. Spread over the duck and leave to marinate in the refrigerator for 4 hours or overnight, turning occasionally.

2　Place the plums in a saucepan with the caster/superfine sugar, white wine vinegar, chilli flakes and cinnamon, and bring to the boil. Simmer gently for 5 minutes, or until the plums have just softened, then leave to cool.

3　Remove the duck from the marinade and pat dry with absorbent kitchen paper. Reserve the marinade. Heat a wok or large frying pan, add the oil and when hot, brown the duck on both sides. Pour in the stock, oyster sauce and reserved marinade, and simmer for 5 minutes. Remove the duck and keep warm.

4　Remove the plums from their liquid and reserve. Pour the liquid into the duck sauce, bring to the boil,and then simmer, uncovered, for 5 minutes, or until reduced and thickened. Arrange the duck on warmed plates. Divide the plums between the plates and spoon over the sauce. Garnish with parsley and serve immediately with noodles.

Roasted Lamb with Rosemary & Garlic

Serves 6

1.6 kg/3½ lb leg of lamb
8 garlic cloves, peeled
few sprigs of fresh rosemary
salt and freshly ground
   black pepper

4 slices pancetta
4 tbsp olive oil
4 tbsp red wine vinegar
6 medium potatoes (about
   900 g/2 lb)
1 large onion

fresh rosemary sprigs,
   to garnish
freshly cooked ratatouille,
   to serve

1 Preheat oven to 200°C/400°F/Gas Mark 6, 15 minutes before roasting. Wipe the leg of lamb with a clean damp cloth, then place the lamb in a large roasting tin. With a sharp knife, make small, deep incisions into the meat. Cut 2–3 garlic cloves into small slivers, then insert with a few small sprigs of rosemary into the lamb. Season to taste with salt and pepper and cover the lamb with the slices of pancetta.

2 Drizzle over 1 tablespoon of the olive oil and lay a few more rosemary sprigs across the lamb. Roast in the preheated oven for 30 minutes, then pour over the vinegar.

3 Peel the potatoes and cut into large dice. Peel the onion and cut into thick wedges, and then thickly slice the remaining garlic. Arrange around the lamb. Pour the remaining olive oil over the potatoes, then reduce the oven temperature to 180°C/ 350°F/Gas Mark 4 and roast for a further 1 hour, or until the lamb is tender. Garnish with fresh rosemary sprigs and serve immediately with the roast potatoes and ratatouille.

Stir-Fried Chicken with Spinach, Tomatoes & Pine Nuts

Serves 4

50 g/2 oz/½ cup pine nuts

2 tbsp sunflower oil

1 red onion, peeled and
　finely chopped

450 g/1 lb skinless, boneless
　chicken breast fillets,
　cut into strips

26 (450 g/1 lb/4 cups) halved
　cherry tomatoes

225 g/8 oz/8 cups baby
　spinach, washed

salt and freshly ground
　black pepper

¼ tsp freshly grated nutmeg

2 tbsp balsamic vinegar

50 g/2 oz/⅓ cup raisins

freshly cooked ribbon noodles
　tossed in butter, to serve

1　Heat the wok and add the pine nuts. Dry-fry for about 2 minutes, shaking often to ensure
　that they toast but do not burn. Remove and reserve. Wipe any dust from the wok.

2　Heat the wok again, add the oil and when hot, add the red onion and stir-fry for 2
　minutes. Add the chicken and stir-fry for 2–3 minutes until golden brown.
　Reduce the heat, toss in the cherry tomatoes and stir-fry gently until the tomatoes
　start to disintegrate.

3　Add the baby spinach and stir-fry for 2–3 minutes until they start to wilt. Season to taste
　with salt and pepper, then sprinkle in the grated nutmeg and drizzle in the balsamic
　vinegar. Finally, stir in the raisins and reserved toasted pine nuts. Serve immediately on
　a bed of buttered ribbon noodles.

Pad Thai

Serves 4

225 g/½ lb flat rice noodles

2 tbsp vegetable oil

225 g/½ lb boneless chicken
breast, skinned, thinly sliced

4 shallots, peeled and
thinly sliced

2 garlic cloves, peeled and
finely chopped

4 spring onions, trimmed and cut
into 2-inch pieces

350 g/¾ lb fresh white crab
meat or tiny prawns/shrimp

75 g/3 oz/1½ cups fresh
beansprouts, rinsed
and drained

2 tbsp preserved or fresh
radish, chopped

2–3 tbsp roasted peanuts,
chopped (optional)

1 red chilli, deseeded and
thinly sliced

For the sauce:

3 tbsp Thai fish sauce (nam pla)

2–3 tbsp rice vinegar or
cider vinegar

1 tbsp chilli bean or
oyster sauce

1 tbsp light brown sugar

1 tbsp toasted sesame oil

1 To make the sauce, whisk all the sauce ingredients in a bowl and reserve. Put the rice noodles in a large bowl and pour over enough hot water to cover. Leave to stand for about 15 minutes until softened. Drain and rinse, then drain again.

2 Heat the oil in a wok over a high heat until hot, but not smoking. Add the chicken strips and stir-fry constantly until they begin to colour. Using a slotted spoon, transfer to a plate. Reduce the heat to medium-high. Add the shallots, garlic and spring onions/scallions, and stir-fry for 1 minute. Stir in the rice noodles and then the reserved sauce; mix well.

3 Add the reserved chicken strips, with the crab meat or prawns/shrimp, beansprouts and radish, and stir well. Cook for about 5 minutes, stirring frequently, until heated through. If the noodles begin to stick, add a little water. Turn into a large shallow serving dish and sprinkle with the chopped peanuts, if desired. Serve immediately.

Teriyaki Salmon

Serves 4

450 g/1 lb salmon fillet, skinned

6 tbsp Japanese teriyaki sauce

1 tbsp rice wine vinegar

1 tbsp tomato paste

dash of Tabasco sauce

2 tsp grated lemon zest

salt and freshly ground
   black pepper

4 tbsp groundnut/peanut oil

1 carrot, peeled and cut into
   matchsticks

125 g/4½ oz/1 cup mangetout/
   snow peas

125 g/4½ oz/1¾ cups oyster
   mushrooms, wiped

1 Using a sharp knife, cut the salmon into thick slices and place in a shallow dish. Mix together the teriyaki sauce, rice wine vinegar, tomato paste, Tabasco sauce, lemon zest and seasoning.

2 Spoon the marinade over the salmon. Cover loosely and leave to marinate in the refrigerator for 30 minutes, turning the salmon or spooning the marinade occasionally over the salmon.

3 Heat a large wok, then add 2 tablespoons of the oil until almost smoking. Stir-fry the carrot for 2 minutes, then add the mangetout/snow peas and stir-fry for a further 2 minutes. Add the oyster mushrooms and stir-fry for 4 minutes, or until softened. Using a slotted spoon, transfer the vegetables to four warmed serving plates and keep warm.

4 Remove the salmon from the marinade, reserving both the salmon and marinade. Add the remaining oil to the wok, heat until almost smoking and cook the salmon for 4–5 minutes, turning once during cooking, until the fish is just flaking. Add the marinade and heat through for 1 minute. Serve immediately, with the salmon arranged on top of the vegetables and the marinade drizzled over.

Desserts

It may seem a little strange to have a dessert section in a vinegar cookery chapter. However, there are a few recipes where the addition of vinegar plays an important role. Perhaps the most notable is the Fluffy Meringue, where it has been used to ensure that the meringue has just the correct amount of soft fluffy, marshmallow texture that is required. Vinegar also works wonders for other desserts, helping to intensify the flavours of both raw and cooked fruits.

Fluffy Meringue

2 medium/large egg whites
100 g/4 oz/½ cup caster/
   superfine sugar

1 tsp raspberry vinegar
1 tsp vanilla extract

Adding vinegar to meringue makes it fluffier and helps prevent it collapsing from being overbeaten. Although only a little vinegar is used here, it is surprising what a difference it makes.

1 Preheat the oven to 150°C/300°F/Gas Mark 2 and line a baking sheet with nonstick baking paper. Mark an 18 cm/7-inch circle on the paper.

2 Whisk the egg whites until stiff, and then gradually whisk in the sugar a spoonful at a time. When all the sugar has been added, stir in the vinegar with the vanilla extract.

3 Place in the centre of the drawn circle and shape into a large case. Bake in the preheated oven for 1½ hours or until set and firm to the touch. Remove from the oven and leave until cold before using or storing in an airtight container.

Mango Sorbet

Serves 6

2 large ripe mangos

2 tbsp white wine vinegar

4–5 tbsp icing sugar, or to taste

1 medium/large egg white

Other fruits can be used for this recipe, if liked – try ripe papaya or one of the many varieties of melon. Whichever you use, do ensure that the fruits are ripe to get the maximum flavour.

1　Turn the freezer to rapid freeze. Peel, stone and then roughly chop the mango flesh. Place in a food processor with the vinegar and sugar, and then blend to a purée.

2　Scrape into a container and freeze for 4 hours or until semifrozen. Whisk the egg white until stiff and stir into the sorbet. Return to the freezer and continue to freeze for 1–2 hours. Allow to soften for 15–30 minutes before serving in scoops.

Balsamic-flavoured Strawberries

Give your guests a surprise by not telling them what you have sprinkled over the fruit and see how many guess.

Hull and lightly rinse large strawberries and cut in half or quarters. Place in a glass bowl. Pour over 2–3 tablespoons balsamic vinegar. Allow to stand for 1–5 minutes. Sprinkle with 1–2 tablespoons caster (superfine) sugar. Stir and serve with ice cream or cream.

More Dessert Tips

- Try adding a teaspoon of vinegar to jelly to give a firmer set.

- Paint a little vinegar over a pie crust for extra shine.

- Give extra tang to a lemon tart with a few drops of vinegar.

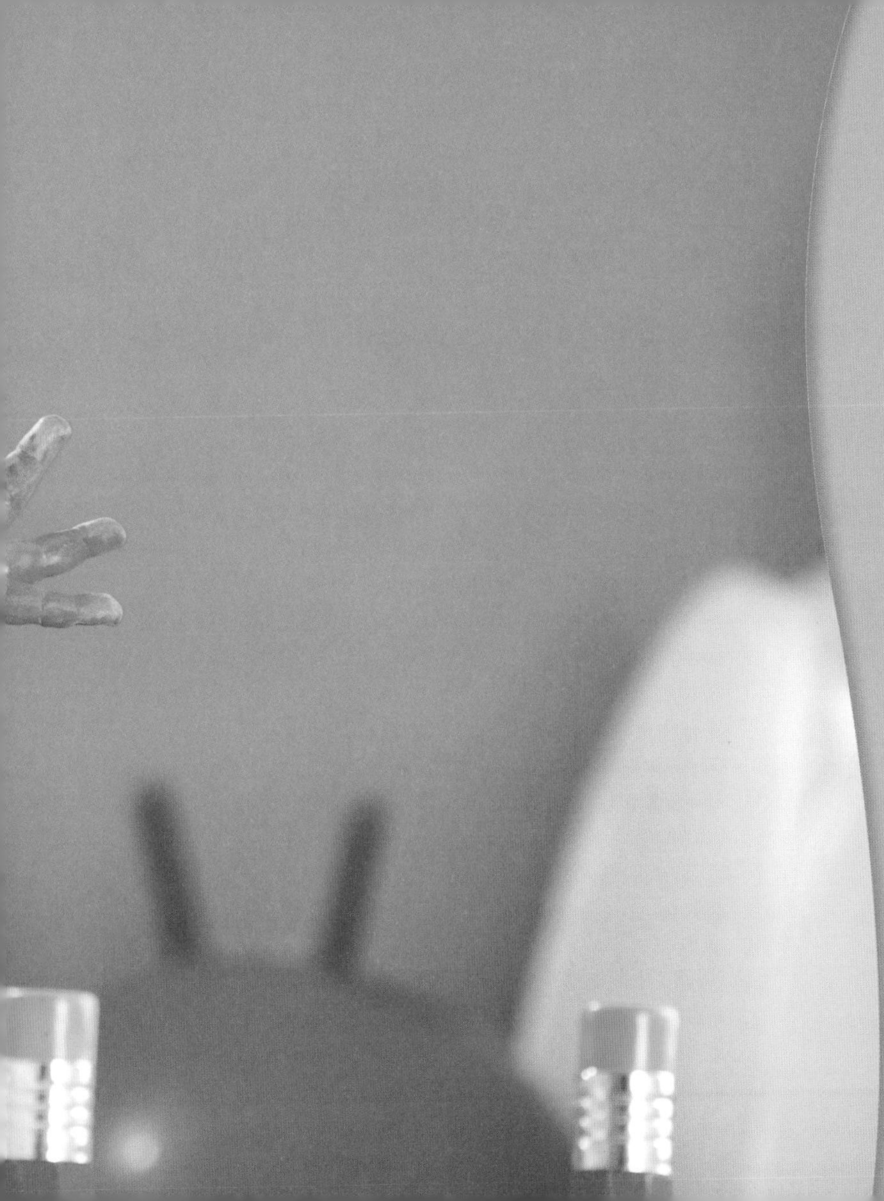

KIDS' STUFF

Fun Science for Kids

On a rainy day when children cannot play in the garden or go to the park, amaze and amuse them with some fun science and activities. All of the experiments here are safe and use household items that are probably already in your kitchen cupboards. They are a great way to learn about chemistry, physics and even about the environment.

Coloured Easter Eggs

This is great for kids of all ages. You can either hard or soft boil the eggs for a fun breakfast or snack, or use 'blown' eggshells made as follows: take a medium size egg and gently pierce a hole in each end with a safety pin; blow hard through one hole so the egg comes out of the other.

To make the paint, mix 1 teaspoon vinegar with each ½ cup of hot water, then add a few drops of food colouring. (Check the food dye bottles for specific amounts.) Vinegar keeps the food dyes bright and prevents streaky, uneven colours.

Berry Ink

Learn how artists in the Middle Ages made inks for manuscripts. All you need is a handful of ripe (or overripe) berries (blueberries, cherries, blackberries, strawberries, elderberries, raspberries, etc.), ½ teaspoon vinegar and ½ teaspoon salt. Fill a strainer with the berries and hold it over a bowl. Using the rounded back of a wooden spoon, crush the berries against the strainer so that the berry juice strains into the bowl.

Keep adding berries until most of their juice has been strained out and only pulp remains. Add the salt and vinegar to the berry juice. The vinegar helps the ink retain its colour and the salt keeps it from getting too mouldy. If the berry ink is too thick, add a tablespoon of water. Store in a jar with a screw-top lid. Only make a small amount of berry ink at a time and, when not in use, keep it tightly covered.

Inflate a Balloon

Using a funnel, add 3 teaspoons bicarbonate of soda (baking soda) to a balloon. Fill a small, clean bottle ⅓ full with vinegar. Carefully holding the neck of the balloon – and without letting any of the bicarbonate of soda fall into the bottle – fit the balloon over the neck of the bottle. Now hold up the balloon so the bicarbonate of soda (baking soda) falls into the vinegar. Watch as the two mix in the bottle to make carbon dioxide, which inflates the balloon.

Volcanic Eruption

This is another fun way to see the chemical reaction of vinegar and bicarbonate of soda (baking soda).

You will need:

720 g/½ lb/6 cups flour
600 g/1⅓ lb/2 cups salt
4 tbsp cooking oil
460 ml/¾ pt/2 cups water
warm water
empty pop or water bottle
red food colouring
washing-up liquid
2 tbsp bicarbonate of soda (baking soda)
vinegar

1   First, make the 'cone' of the volcano. Mix together the flour, salt, cooking oil and water. The resulting mixture should be a smooth, firm dough (add more water if needed).

2   Stand a pop or water bottle in a baking tray and mould the dough around it into a volcano shape. Fill up the bottle most of the way with warm water (adding a drop or two of red food colouring will make a great 'lava' effect!).

3   Add 6 drops of washing-up liquid to the bottle contents. Add the bicarbonate of soda (baking soda) to the liquid. Slowly pour in some vinegar (do not waste expensive balsamic vinegar though!) into the bottle and watch the volcano erupt!

Mini Rocket

This is a fun experiment to try for Fireworks Night.

You will need:

scissors

plastic shopping bag or coloured tissue paper

an old cork – you will need one that fits snugly into your bottle

glue

empty pop or water bottle

120 ml/4 fl oz/½ cup water

120 ml/4 fl oz/½ cup vinegar

paper towel

1 tsp bicarbonate of soda (baking soda)

 CAUTION: Be sure to stand well away from the direction of the flying cork.

1   Cut up the plastic bag or coloured tissue paper into a few thin 'shreds' to make streamers, and glue the streamers on to one end of the cork.

2   Take a small, clean pop or water bottle and pour in the water and vinegar.

3   Next, take a paper towel and put the bicarbonate of soda (baking soda) in the centre, twisting the ends to stop the bicarbonate from falling out.

4   Take the bottle outside, drop in the paper towel with the bicarbonate in it and put the cork on tight. Stand back and watch the carbon dioxide gas force the cork (with its streamers) out of the bottle.

Bendy Bones

This is a great way to show kids the importance of calcium in their diet to build healthy bones and teeth. Take a chicken bone and place it in a screw-top jar of vinegar tightly sealed for a day or so – get your kids to handle the bone before the experiment so they can feel the hardness. When you take the bone out of the vinegar, it will be bendy and rubbery. Why? The vinegar has dissolved the calcium in the bone, making it weak and bendy.

Why We Need to Brush our Teeth

This experiment takes a couple of days, but is a great way to show kids the importance of teeth brushing: eggshells and teeth can both be weakened by acids but protection can be given by fluoride toothpaste. Here's how to do it: take 2 fresh eggs with no cracks in the shells and place one in a jar full of vinegar (a weak acid similar to that which causes tooth cavities) and put the lid on. You will soon start to see bubbles form on the eggshell as the acid begins to work dissolving the calcium.

Take the other egg and carefully smear a good layer of fluoride toothpaste all over the shell, making sure there are no gaps or air bubbles in the toothpaste. Put this egg into a jar filled with vinegar and put the lid on. Let both eggs sit for about 4 days, and then gently lift the eggs out of the jars. The 'unprotected egg' will be very fragile because the acid has eaten into the calcium in the eggshell. Gently rinse off the toothpaste from the 'protected egg' and see how the shell has remained hard thanks to the protective layer of fluoride toothpaste.

Further Reading

Alderton, D. et al., *The Complete Book of Pets and Pet Care*, Lorenz Books, 2006

Andrews, G., *100 Science Experiments*, Usborne Publishing Ltd, 2009

Briggs, M., *Vinegar: 1001 Practical Uses*, Abbeydale Press, 2006

Constantino, M., *Household Hints*, Flame Tree Publishing, 2009

Corkhill, M., *Self-Sufficiency: Natural Remedies*, New Holland Publishers Ltd, 2011

Franklin, L., *Oils and Vinegars*, Ryland, Peters & Small Ltd, 2008

Gabriel, J., *The Green Beauty Guide*, Health Communications, 2008

Good Housekeeping, *Easy to Make! Salads and Dressings*, Collins & Brown, 2008

Harrison, J., *Easy Jams, Chutneys and Preserves*, Right Way, 2009

Harrison, J., *Low-Cost Living: Live Better, Spend Less*, Right Way, 2009

Mindell, E.L. with Johns, L.M., *Amazing Apple Cider Vinegar: A Good Health Guide*, Keats Publishing, 1997

Moore, M., *Vim & Vinegar: Hundreds of Ingenious Household Uses*, HarperCollins, 2005

Orey, C., *The Healing Powers of Vinegar*, Kensington Publishing Corporation, 2009

Reader's Digest, *How to Clean Just About Anything: Ingenious Secrets for a Fresh and Sparkling Home*, Reader's Digest, 2006

Stanway, P., *The Miracle of Cider Vinegar*, Watkins Publishing, 2010

Strauss, R., *Self-Sufficiency: Household Cleaning*, New Holland Publishers Ltd, 2009

Sutherland, D. and J., *Bicarbonate of Soda: Hundreds of Household Uses*, Flame Tree Publishing, 2011

Vukovic, L., *1001 Natural Remedies*, Dorling Kindersley, 2003

Websites

www.allotment-garden.org
A website that offers gardening advice as well as a recipe section which includes many preserves and chutney suggestions.

www.h2g2.com
This website encourages people to share their advice and insight on just about anything, as well as ask for help.

www.bbc.co.uk/food/vinegar
A website offering ideas for recipes using vinegar, for a variety of occasions.

www.greenlivingtips.com
A website that offers tips on green living for every aspect of your life, as well as a free newsletter.

www.heinzvinegar.com
The official website for Heinz vinegar. It offers recipe suggestions and recommendations for vinegar's uses around the house.

www.hintsandthings.co.uk
A website that provides a vast number of household hints categorized by the various rooms of the home.

www.home-remedies-for-you.com
A website that suggests cures and treatments made with natural ingredients, which you can make at home.

www.hygieneexpert.co.uk
A website that offers hygiene information for adults, children and pets.

www.sciencekids.co.nz
A website that provides a fun environment for children to learn about science through quizzes and experiments, some of which involve vinegar.

www.the-apple-cider-vinegar-company.com
A producer of apple cider vinegar, with 'mother' intact, available to buy worldwide.

www.versatilevinegar.org/uses-tips
A website that covers all aspects of vinegar information, from its history and market trends, to its practical applications.

www.vinegartips.com
A website that offers numerous suggestions on how to utilize vinegar.

Picture Credits

The following images are © **Flame Tree Publishing Ltd**: 6, 8, 22 & 102, 33, 35, 38, 40, 47, 48 & 51, 54 & 61, 56, 57, 60 & 63, 62, 65, 66, 68, 69, 70, 73, 81, 83, 98, 106 & 113, 108, 110, 116 & 121, 123, 128, 164, 168, 176 & 192, 177, 178, 179, 186, 190, 200b, 202, 204, 206–228, 231, 232, 240, 242, 245. All other images are courtesy of **Shutterstock** and © the following photographers: 1 & 175 vgm; 3 & 136 lognetic; 4t & 28 Aleksej Starostin; 4b & 104 Gr8; 4c & 52 Thomas M Perkins; 5b & 236 Alena Ozerova; 5c & 134 Deklofenak; 5t & 124 Nikoner; 7 Igor Smichkov; 11 StockLite; 12 Natalia Clarke; 14 Mirka Markova; 15 Katharina Wittfeld; 17 Igor Normann; 19 Gianluca Figliola Fantini; 21 michael rubin; 23, 189 marco mayer; 24 wonderisland; 25 Subbotina Anna; 27 Krzysztof Slusarczyk; 30 & 41 Tihis; 31 zulufoto; 37 Péter Gudella; 39 maska; 42 Dmitriy Yakovlev; 43 Jennifer Nickert; 45 Masyanya; 49, 140 Kurhan; 55 olly; 59 Pavelis; 67 DJM-photo; 71 haveseen; 75 Jeffrey Van Daele; 82 Andrew Kerr; 84 clearviewstock; 85 Stephen VanHorn; 86 & 91 Andrey Stratilatov; 87, 138 DUSAN ZIDAR; 89 Eva Gruendemann; 92 Graeme Dawes; 94 & 97 sharon kingston; 95 Tischenko Irina; 99 Kameel4u; 100 Jiri; 101 Patrick McCall; 103 photovaruj; 107 Gordon Swanson; 109 Julija Sapic ; 111 Ronald Sumners; 112 Damian Herde; 115 Tero Sivula; 117 Ellen Morgan; 118 Elena Elisseeva; 119 Orientaly; 122 Svetlana Turilova; 126 & 129 Joy Brown; 127 Spauln; 131 tepic; 132 Alice Mary Herden/Vision-Vault LLC; 133 Steve Collender; 137 Jakub Semeniuk; 139 accesslab; 141 Scruggelgreen; 143 kuzmichs; 144 & 149 Ximagination; 145 Kanwarjit Singh Boparai; 147 Lasse Kristensen; 148 Danny Smythe; 151 Levent Konuk; 153 Khafizov Ivan Harisovich; 155 Michael Pettigrew; 157 Gordon Ball LRPS; 158 Valua Vitaly; 159 MalibuBooks; 160 glennebo; 161 Yuri Arcurs; 163 wavebreakmedia ltd; 165, 188 & 199 Monkey Business Images; 167 Goodluz; 169 suravid; 170 Josh Resnick; 172 & 174 Christopher Elwell; 173 SunnyS; 180 & 187, 238 & 247 Elena Schweitzer; 181 Marina Nabatova; 183 Elke Dennis; 185 Liv friis-larsen; 191 Patty Orly; 193 Robyn Mackenzie; 194 Nadja Antonova; 195 Tobik; 197 CCat82; 200t Alex Staroseltsev; 201 Denis Vrublevski; 203 ep_stock; 205 jordache; 233 Kheng Guan Toh; 234 Ildi Papp; 235 Ingrid Balabanova; 239 DenisNata; 241 Mny-Jhee; 243 Africa Studio; 244 Ferenc Szelepcsenyi; 246 valzan; 248 Timothy Geiss; 249 Gorilla; 251 Linda Muir. Illustrations © Elena Akimova (bottles), bioraven (household items) and Epine (honey).

Index

Recipes are indicated
by upper case initials.

A

acetic acid 9, 10, 14, 30, 54, 106, 156
acid soil 108–10
age spots 160
animal repellent 112–14
ants 114
apple cider vinegar 20, 136–42, 144, 158
Apricot, Mango and Cranberry Chutney 202
astringent 158, 160
athlete's foot 150–52
awnings 118

B

Babylonians 6
bactericide 30, 36, 40, 54, 60, 64, 70, 72, 74, 90, 128, 130, 138, 140, 162, 176
balloons, inflating 242
balsamic vinegar 18, 180
Balsamic Flavoured Strawberries 234
bathrooms 70–74
baths 74

BBQ Sauce 196
beer vinegar 16
Beetroot & Potato Medley 208
berry ink 240–42
berry stains 66
Bible 6
bins 120
bird droppings 120
bird feeders 128
black spot 112
blankets 42
bleaching 36
blinds, Venetian 82
bloodstains 32–34
bones, bendy 248
brass polish 56
brick 94, 100–102
bruises 158, 160

C

calluses 148
can openers 64
candle wax 58
cane vinegar 24–26
car cleaning 122
carpet stains 84
cat repellent 112–14
cats' bowls 130
ceiling cleaning 98

cement burns 102
cement painting 102
champagne vinegar 16–18
chest congestion 146
chicken
  Pad Thai 224
  Stir-fried Chicken with Spinach, Tomatoes & Pine Nuts 222
  Warm Chicken & Potato Salad with Peas & Mint 214
children 238, 248
china 62
cider vinegar see apple cider vinegar
Cleopatra 8, 172
closets 88
clothes
  clothes smells 38–40
  colour maintenance 46
coconut vinegar 24
cold sores 150
colds 146
collars 34
concrete burns 102
cooking smells 88
copper polish 56
corn sugar vinegar 26
corns 148

Cranberry, Apricot and Mango Chutney 202
creases, sharp 50
Crème Fraîche Dressing 194
cuffs 34
culinary tips 176–78
cuticle softener 168
cutting boards 62–64
cutting tools 100

D

dandruff 164
date vinegar 22
de-icers 122
decking 118
deglazing pans 178
deodorant 162
deodorant stains 32
deodorizing car mats 122
desserts 232, 234
diaper rash 152
digestion 156
dishcloths 66
dishwashers 68
dogs' drinking water 130
drains 120
dressings 188
  Classic Vinaigrette 190
  Crème Fraîche Dressing 194

duck
  Seared Duck with Pickled
    Plums 218
dust 98

E

eggs
  Easter egg decorating 240
  perfect poached eggs 176
  preventing cracks in boiled
    eggs 176

F

fabric softeners 42
fabrics, restoring white
    36, 46
  wrinkled 44
fish
  Salmon Ceviche 200
  Teriyaki Salmon 226
flasks 66
flavoured vinegars 26, 180
flavouring foods 178
fleas 126, 132
floors 84
flu 146
fly traps 114
food containers 64–66
food smells 88
footwear 88–90
fridges 68
fried foods 178
fruit flies 90

fruit vinegar 22
furniture 76, 78–80, 118

G

garden furniture 118
gardening 106
germs 54, 72, 176
glasses 62
gold jewellery 56
grease stains 62
greasy food 178
greasy walls 96
grill pans 64
grout 74

H

hair
  blonde hair 164
  hair conditioner 166
Hannibal 8, 172
head lice 166
hiccups 156
Hippocrates 6, 172
history 6–9
Hollandaise Sauce 192
honey vinegar 24

I

ink spots 34–36
insect bites 154
  pets 132
insects 90, 114
ironing 48–50
itching 152–54

K

kettles, de-scaling 68
kitchens 60
kombucha vinegar 26

L

lace, restoring vintage 36
lamb
  Roasted Lamb with
    Rosemary & Garlic 220
leather furniture 80
lice 166
linoleum 84
lint-free laundry 42

M

making vinegar from
    scratch 174
malt vinegar 14
Mango Sorbet 232
Mango, Apricot and
    Cranberry Chutney 202
marble 80, 94
Mark Antony 8
mealy bugs 114
meat, disinfecting 176
  tenderizing 176
medicinal uses 6, 8–9,
    144–56
Meringue, Fluffy 230
metal 94
  metal cleaner 56
mice 90
microwaves 68

mildew 98, 118
  powdery mildew 112
mini rocket 246
Mint Sauce 198
mosquito bites 154
mould 54
muscles, sore 156

N

nail polish 168
nappy rash 152
noodles
  Pad Thai 224
nuts
  Stir-fried Chicken with
    Spinach, Tomatoes & Pine
    Nuts 222

O

odour removal 86
  closets 88
  clothes smells 38–40
olives 176
onions
  French Onion Tart 210
Orleans method 9–10

P

Pad Thai 224
paint fumes 98
paint splashes on windows
    82
paintbrushes, renovating
    96–98

Panzanella 212
Pasteur, Louis 9
patio umbrellas 118
pets 126
  ear cleaning 132
  insect bites 132
  pet beds 128
  pet dishes 130
  pet messes 130
pewter polish 56
Pickles, Mixed 204
pimples 150
plant food 110
plastering 96
Pliny the Elder 8
plugholes 74
polish build-up 78–80
potatoes
  Beetroot & Potato
    Medley 208
  Warm Chicken & Potato
    Salad with Peas &
    Mint 214
pre-wash stain removal 32
production 9

R
raisin vinegar 22
red clothes 46
red wine vinegar 16
rice vinegar 20
rocket, mini 246
Romans 8
Rose Vinegar 184

Rosemary Vinegar 182
rust on plants 112
rust removal 100

S
salt marks 44
sauces 188
  BBQ Sauce 196
  Hollandaise Sauce 192
  Mint Sauce 198
saws 100
scorch marks 50
scratches in wood 78
scratching posts 132
seeds, germinating 110
shellfish
  Pad Thai 224
sherry vinegar 18–20
shiny seats (skirts and
  trousers) 44
showers 72
  shower curtains 72
  shower heads 74
sinks 74
sinus congestion 146
skin softener 162
skin toner 162
smells see odour removal
smoke smells 88
soil testing 108
sole plate, cleaning 50
Spiced Vinegar 186
spots 150
stains

berry stains 66
bloodstains 32–34
carpet stains 84
deodorant stains 32
grease stains 62
ink spots 34–36
old stains 34
salt marks 44
suede stains 44
wine stains 32
steam iron, flushing 50
steamed puddings 178
sticky labels 58
stone 94
strawberries
  Balsamic Flavoured
    Strawberries 234
suede stains 44
sunburn 152
sweat 162

T
taps 74
teeth brushing 248
throat, sore 146
ticks 126, 132
tiles 72
toenails 168
toilet bowls 74
toilet training, pets 130
tomatoes
  Stir-fried Chicken with
    Spinach, Tomatoes &
    Pine Nuts 222

U
umezu 22
urine 90

V
veins, broken 160
  varicose 148
Venetian blinds 82
Vinaigrette, Classic 190
vinegar mother 9–10, 174
vinyl floors 84
volcanic eruption 244

W
wall cleaning 96, 98
wallpaper stripping 96
warts 150
washing machines 40
wasp stings 154
water rings 78
wax build-up 78–80
weeds 112
white vinegar 14, 30, 54
white wine vinegar 16
windows 82
windscreen wipers 122
wine stains 32
wood 94, 100
  wood cleaning 100
  wood scratches 78
woollens 42